The
Rhodesian
Ridgeback

An Owner's Guide To

A HAPPY HEALTHY PET

Howell Book House

Wiley Publishing, Inc.

Howell Book House

Published by Wiley Publishing, Inc., Hoboken, NJ
Published simultaneously in Canada

Limit of Liability/Disclaimer of Warranty: While the publisher and the author have used their best efforts in preparing this book, they make no representations or warranties with respect to the accuracy or completeness of the contents of this book and specifically disclaim any implied warranties of merchantability or fitness for a particular purpose. No warranty may be created or extended by sales representatives or written sales materials. The advice and strategies contained herein may not be suitable for your situation. You should consult with a professional where appropriate. Neither the publisher nor the author shall be liable for any loss of profit or any other commercial damages, including but not limited to special, incidental, consequential, or other damages.

For general information about our other products and services, please contact our Customer Care Department within the United States at (800) 762-2974, outside the United States at (317) 572-3993 or fax (317) 572-4002.

Wiley also publishes its books in a variety of electronic formats. Some content that appears in print may not be available in electronic books. For more information about Wiley products, visit our web site at www.wiley.com.

Library of Congress Cataloging-in-Publication data

Bailey, Eileen M.
The Rhodesian ridgeback: an owner's guide to a happy healthy pet.
    p.cm
Includes bibliographical references.
ISBN 1-58245-011-0
1. Rhodesian Ridgeback. I. Title
SF429.R5   B35   2000
636.753'6—dc21   99-047512
                CIP

Manufactured in the United States of America
10 9 8 7 6 5 4 3 2

Series Director: Susanna Thomas
Book Design by Michele Laseau
Cover Design by Iris Jeromnimon
External Features Illustration by Shelley Norris
Other Illustrations by Jeff Yesh
Photography:
  Front cover by Mary Bloom
  Back cover by Mary Bloom
  All photography by Mary Bloom unless otherwise noted.
    Joan Balzarini: 96
    Paulette Braun/Pets by Paulette: 96
    Buckinghambill American Cocker Spaniels: 148
    Sian Cox: 134
    Dr. Ian Dunbar: 98, 101, 103, 111, 116–117, 122, 123, 127
    Howell Book House: 24
    Dan Lyons: 96
    Cathy Merrithew: 129
    Liz Palika: 133
    Susan Rezy: 96–97
    Bob Schwartz: 20
    Judith Strom: 96, 107, 110, 128, 130, 135, 137, 139, 140, 144, 149, 150
Production Team: Tammy Ahrens, David Faust, and Heather Pope

Contents

Welcome
to the
World

of the

Rhodesian Ridgeback

External Features of the Rhodesian Ridgeback

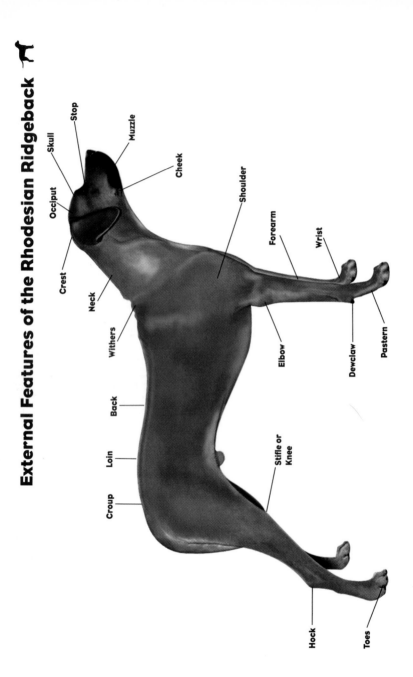

chapter 1

What Is a Rhodesian Ridgeback?

The Rhodesian Ridgeback is courageous enough to face off the fearsome African lion, fast enough to bring down the swift gazelle at full gallop, strong enough to trek many miles across hostile terrain and gentle enough to be the perfect playmate to even the youngest children. He is a unique blend of guardian, companion and hunter that is without an equal in the entire world of dogs.

He carries on his back a distinctive ridge of hair so the observer knows who he is at a glance, and it is a

mark he wears with justifiable pride. Known also as the African Lion Hound, the Rhodesian Ridgeback was developed in the southern portion of the African continent following the emigration of large numbers of Dutch, German and Huguenot settlers. The settlers brought their native European breeds with them and the ensuing matings between many of these and dogs of the Hottentot people evolved into the modern Rhodesian Ridgeback. Those early Ridgebacks filled the farmers' need for a dog that could work on the farm, help in the hunt and that could stand up to the harsh conditions encountered in the bush.

In 1877 he came to the attention of several celebrated big-game hunters, and was made famous for his extreme courage in harassing and holding at bay the King of Beasts. He has the reputation of being the only breed of dog that will take on a lion and live to remember it. The Ridgeback's courage is legendary. But even more remarkable is the breed's versatility.

The Rhodesian Ridgeback belongs to the group of dogs known as hounds. The American Kennel Club Hound Group is composed of dogs developed to

The Rhodesian Ridgeback was developed to meet a unique need in a harsh, pioneer environment.

hunt furred game and whose primary function is to bring the hunter within range of his prey. The hounds are classified into two main branches. The scent-hounds track prey by using their exceptional noses to follow the trail of the game. The sighthounds, or gaze-hounds, hunt by visually tracking their prey and running it down with amazing swiftness. The Rhodesian Ridgeback is a link between the two divisions that does both. His body type is not like the ponderous, loose-skinned, long-eared scent hounds, such as the Bloodhound or Basset Hound. Nor is it the sinewy leanness of the gazehounds, like the Greyhound or the Whippet, breeds built for extreme speed. Rather, the Ridgeback is a sleek, tight-skinned dog of substantial bone and muscle who is capable of tracking his target through the thick African scrub, flushing it into the open and either running it down or holding it at bay until the hunter arrives. In addition, all the years that the Rhodesian Ridgeback served as a guardian and companion gave him a legacy of watchfulness, devotion to his family and resourcefulness that makes him so highly regarded as a companion today.

The Breed Standard

WHAT IS A BREED STANDARD?

The specific attributes of each recognized dog breed identify that breed and distinguish it from every other. These attributes are detailed for each breed in the Official Standard.

The breed Standard is a written picture of the conceptually perfect Rhodesian Ridgeback. Much like a cookbook, the breed Standard describes the various ingredients which, when combined properly, create an unparalleled whole. Unlike a cookbook however, the breed Standard describes an ideal which is to be as closely approximated as possible. To actually achieve the perfection it presents is the elusive goal of conscientious breeders everywhere, who may spend a lifetime in pursuit of it.

The original breed Standard for the Rhodesian Ridgeback was first written in 1922 in South Africa. The Standard in effect in the United States today is presented below. This Standard was written by the Rhodesian Ridgeback Club of the United States and approved by the

---

THE AMERICAN KENNEL CLUB

Familiarly referred to as "the AKC," the American Kennel Club is a nonprofit organization devoted to the advancement of purebred dogs. The AKC maintains a registry of recognized breeds and adopts and enforces rules for dog events including shows, obedience trials, field trials, hunting tests, lure coursing, herding, earthdog trials, agility and the Canine Good Citizen program. It is a club of clubs, established in 1884 and composed, today, of over 500 autonomous dog clubs throughout the United States. Each club is represented by a delegate; the delegates make up the legislative body of the AKC, voting on rules and electing directors. The AKC maintains the Stud Book—the record of every dog ever registered with the AKC—and publishes a variety of materials on purebred dogs, including a monthly magazine, books and numerous educational pamphlets. For more information, contact the AKC at the address listed in Chapter 13, "Resources," and look for the names of their publications in Chapter 12, "Recommended Reading."

American Kennel Club (AKC) in 1955, changing very little since the original was drawn up. It creates an excellent visual image of the dog it describes. The breed Standard is printed in italics, with interpretation and comments following in roman text. For any questions regarding points of anatomy, please refer to the illustration at the beginning of this chapter that depicts these points.

The Rhodesian Ridgeback's temperament and conformation suited him to his role as a guard dog and hunter of large game. Today, he makes a wonderful companion for any active owner.

GENERAL APPEARANCE

The Ridgeback represents a strong, muscular and active dog, symmetrical and balanced in outline. A mature Ridgeback is a handsome, upstanding and athletic dog, capable of great endurance with a fair (good) amount of speed. Of even, dignified temperament, the Ridgeback is devoted and affectionate to his master, reserved with strangers. The peculiarity of this breed is the ridge on the back. The ridge must be regarded as the characteristic feature of the breed.

Keep this picture in mind at all times when considering the overall picture of a typical Rhodesian Ridgeback.

SIZE, PROPORTION, SUBSTANCE

A mature Ridgeback should be symmetrical in outline, slightly longer than tall but well balanced. Dogs—25 to 27 inches in height; Bitches—24 to 26 inches in height. Desirable weight: Dogs—85 pounds; Bitches—70 pounds.

The Ridgeback is a medium to large dog combining power, grace and beauty. He needs to be fast and agile; too much height, or too much weight in muscle and bone inhibits speed and agility. The Ridgeback that was too heavy did not survive long in the harsh African environment. On the other hand, a Ridgeback should not be so small or slight as to lack endurance and strength, nor should he lack the size necessary to deal with large and dangerous adversaries.

HEAD

Should be of fair length, the skull flat and rather broad between the ears and should be free from wrinkles when in repose. The stop should be reasonably well defined.

The Ridgeback's head should fit his body and be powerful in appearance but free from coarseness or heaviness. The apparent strength should be tempered with a look of elegance, imparting dignity and intelligence to the dog. The Ridgeback's head should never appear too small or too heavy for his body and should always be in harmonious proportion. A head that is reminiscent of a Mastiff, or in the other extreme, of a Greyhound, is incorrect. Because the breed is relatively young, there are several different head types, all of which are acceptable, providing they adhere to the above Standard. The width of the back skull between the base of the ears should be equal to its

This dog represents a splendid example of correct breed type.

length from occiput to stop. When the dog is alert, wrinkles on the forehead become visible and add greatly to the Ridgeback's expression. When the dog is relaxed, the wrinkles disappear. The head should be in keeping with the sex of the dog: Dogs should be masculine and bitches should be feminine.

Eyes

Should be moderately well apart and should be round, bright and sparkling with intelligent expression, their color harmonizing with the color of the dog.

A small or elliptically shaped eye is incorrect; keen eyesight was important to survival, and the eyes should be of good size. The eye should never bulge out, which would make it prone to injury. Neither should it be recessed or hidden beneath skin or bone. The skin surrounding the eyes should be tight. A dog with a black nose and pigment should also have a dark eye. The eye color may match the dog's coat color or be darker; it should never be lighter than the coat. A dog with a brown or liver nose and pigment may have amber eyes; the eye color may or may not be lighter than the coat color in this instance.

Ears

Should be set rather high, of medium size, rather wide at the base and tapering to a rounded point. They should be carried close to the head.

The length of the ear should fall just short of the rear edge of the dog's mouth when pulled forward along the jaw. The ears should not be creased or folded. A Ridgeback's ears are very expressive of the dog's mood.

Muzzle

Should be long, deep and powerful. The lips clean, closely fitting the jaws.

The Ridgeback has a dry mouth and does not drool. When viewed from the side, the end of the muzzle should appear to be squared off. The under jaw should not slope away from the bite, but should be full and powerful. The length of the muzzle from stop to nose tip should equal the length of the back skull from stop to occiput.

Nose

Should be black, brown or liver, in keeping with the color of the dog. No other colored nose is permissible. A black nose should be accompanied by dark eyes, a brown or liver nose with amber eyes.

The pigment of the eye rims and lips will match the color of the dog's nose. Although the black nose is more frequently seen, dogs with brown or liver noses are strikingly beautiful as well. Dogs of all pigments can occur in a wide range of wheaten shades as specified in the color section of the breed Standard.

WHAT IS A BREED STANDARD?

A breed standard—a detailed description of an individual breed—is meant to portray the ideal specimen of that breed. This includes structure, temperament, gait, type—all aspects of the dog. Because the standard describes an ideal specimen, it isn't based on any particular dog. It is a concept against which judges compare actual dogs and breeders strive to produce dogs. At a dog show, the dog that wins is the one that comes closest, in the judge's opinion, to the standard for its breed. Breed standards are written by the breed parent clubs, the national organizations formed to oversee the well-being of the breed. They are voted on and approved by the members of the parent clubs.

Bite

*Jaws level and strong with well-developed teeth, especially the
canines or holders. Scissors bite preferred.*

When the upper front incisors tightly overlap the lower
front incisors and the upper and lower canine teeth
mesh snugly, the formation is called a scissors bite. The
Ridgeback must be able to find and maintain a good
grip on his prey, lest he become its dinner! A weak jaw
or defective teeth could easily affect a dog's survival.

NECK, TOPLINE, BODY

*The neck should be fairly strong and free from throatiness.
The chest should not be too wide, but very deep and capacious,
ribs moderately well sprung, never rounded like barrel hoops
(which would indicate want of speed). The back is powerful
and firm with strong loins which are muscular and slightly*

*When in
motion, the
Ridgeback's tail
should be car-
ried with a
slight curve.*

*arched. The tail should be strong at
the insertion and generally tapering
towards the end, free from coarseness.
It should not be inserted too high or
too low and should be carried with a
slight curve upwards, never curled
or gay.*

The neck and back should be
powerful and muscular. Excess
skin that could easily be caught or
torn is to be avoided. A long back
or sloping topline is not sufficiently strong to carry a dog all
day through difficult conditions. Remember that the
Ridgeback should be *slightly* longer than he is tall. An
arched and muscular loin lends strength and flexibility
to the back. The chest should not be wide like that of
a working dog, nor should it be narrow like that of a
sighthound, but should be well filled between the
shoulders. The chest, however, should not be so full as
to inhibit correct front movement. The depth of chest,
when viewed from the side, should reach fully to the
level of the dog's elbow. The chest cavity should allow
for ample heart and lung room. The tail should be
powerful as well since it acts as a balance for the dog in

motion. The Ridgeback has a saber tail, which may be carried down in a loose "S" curve, or may be carried not more than a few inches above the level of the back while the dog is in motion.

FOREQUARTERS

The shoulders should be sloping, clean and muscular, denoting speed. Elbows close to the body. The forelegs should be perfectly straight, strong and heavy in bone. The feet should be compact with well-arched toes, round, tough, elastic pads, protected by hair between the toes and pads. Dewclaws may be removed.

HINDQUARTERS

In the hind legs the muscles should be clean, well defined and hocks well down. Feet as in front.

Both the fore- and hindquarters of a Rhodesian Ridgeback are extremely important. Bone must be heavy enough to withstand the punishment of rough traveling conditions, as well as the running, jumping and fast turns made during the chase. The feet and toes must be able to grip and push as well, and must be able to withstand considerable punishment over all kinds of surfaces. A flat foot is to be avoided. The shoulder should have sufficient length of upper arm to enable a free, ground-covering stride, while the hocks should be set low enough to match the shoulder with strong drive from behind. A rear with too much angulation loses strength. The Ridgeback is a dog of moderate angles both fore and aft. The major muscles should be easily apparent but should not bulge grossly.

COAT

Should be short and dense, sleek and glossy in appearance but neither woolly nor silky.

The Ridgeback coat feels prickly to the touch when rubbed in the wrong direction. The coat is tight to the skin and flat in all areas except along the ridge where the hair growth changes direction.

COLOR

Light wheaten to red wheaten. A little white on the chest and toes permissible but excessive white there, on the belly, or above the toes is undesirable.

Wheaten is defined as pale buff or gold, like the color of ripe wheat or champagne. Acceptable shades range from pale to dark into wheaten with red tones, called red wheaten, up through a dark red. All these colors are equally permissible, with none favored over the others. Dogs of any pigment can occur in the full spectrum of shades allowed in the breed Standard.

A black-nosed Ridgeback may have a black mask, and a liver-nosed dog may have a brown mask. The mask should be confined to the area of the muzzle, and a dog with a mask may also have dark ears and/or a bit of dark hair around the eyes. There should, however, be a definite break in color between the eyes and the mask on the muzzle; a solid dark face is incorrect.

Note the black mask on the black-nosed dog. The liver-nosed dog has no mask. Both are correct.

White markings are permissible on a Ridgeback, but ideally should be kept to a minimum. There was some debate in years past regarding just how much white is acceptable, but it is now generally agreed that a good dog should not be penalized for white markings that are not too extensive. A current controversy centers on the presence of black hairs in the Ridgeback coat, other than on the area of the mask. Some black-pigmented

Ridgebacks may have a black tail, a black "necklace" around the throat, a black "widow's peak" on the forehead and black hairs sprinkled throughout the body coat. Dark brown or gray hairs in these areas have been seen on liver-pigmented dogs as well. This author believes these markings to be incorrect, but not all fanciers agree. At this time, the American Standard is the only one that allows black hairs in the Ridgeback coat. In all other countries, this is a serious fault.

RIDGE

The hallmark of this breed is the ridge on the back, which is formed by the hair growing in the opposite direction to the rest of the coat. The ridge must be regarded as the characteristic feature of the breed. The ridge should be clearly defined, tapering and symmetrical. It should start immediately behind the shoulders and continue to a point between the prominence of the hips and should contain two identical crowns (whorls) directly opposite each other. The lower edge of the crowns (whorls) should not extend further down the ridge than one third of the ridge. Disqualification: Ridgelessness. Serious Fault: One crown (whorl) or more than two crowns (whorls).

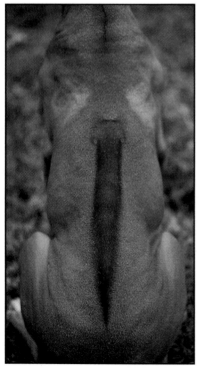

The ridge is the breed's hallmark.

The ridge is the mark above all others that distinguishes this breed. If your pet Ridgeback does not have the perfect ridge described above, he nonetheless shows his unique heritage on his back. Many people are unaware that a Rhodesian Ridgeback can be born without any ridge at all. The dog without a ridge may not immediately be recognizable as a Rhodesian Ridgeback to people unfamiliar with the breed but will still have the other wonderful qualities of the Ridgeback inherent in his ancestry. Dogs with incorrect ridges may participate successfully in all AKC events except conformation shows, as well as racing events. A dog without a ridge may not compete in conformation shows, lure coursing or racing events but may participate in all others, such as obedience and agility trials and tracking tests. You should know when buying a Ridgeback puppy that the ridge does not "grow in" as the pup matures. The ridge he wears as a puppy will be the same ridge he wears as an adult; it will only grow in proportion with the dog.

GAIT

At the trot, the back is held level and the stride is efficient, long, free and unrestricted. Reach and drive expressing a perfect balance between power and elegance. At the chase, the Ridgeback demonstrates great coursing ability and endurance.

The Ridgeback in motion is a truly beautiful sight. At the trot, the Ridgeback covers ground with every stride. The ideal trot appears effortless and smooth. As the trot becomes faster, the feet should converge on the midline in both front and rear; this is called single-tracking, and is the most efficient use of energy for a dog who must travel many miles each day. Although he is not as fast as his sighthound cousins when running, the Ridgeback is very fast when compared to other breeds of his size and weight. Moreover, he can keep running long distances with good speed while other dogs quickly fade. It is the difference between the marathon runner and sprinter. The Rhodesian Ridgeback is very agile even at high speeds, being able to leap and turn in a split second.

TEMPERAMENT

Dignified and even tempered. Reserved with strangers.

The Rhodesian Ridgeback is extremely devoted and loyal to his family. He adores children and is patient, gentle and protective with them. He likes to be close to his people at all times, to the point of sitting or lying very near, or even on top of, their feet. He is not given to growling or displays of aggression, but if bothered by a situation will simply remove himself from it. He is a pack dog who is good with other dogs and pets, provided he is trained to accept them. Cats and other small creatures are normally considered prey, although tolerance can be taught. The Ridgeback has an enormous sense of self, and to those not of his chosen family and friends he presents an aloof and dignified demeanor. While he is openly affectionate to his own people, he does not care to have strangers fawn over him, and will accept caresses with indifference. If a Ridgeback does not care to be admired, he will most often turn his back to intrusive strangers, clearly snubbing them—although this attitude holds true also for other dogs.

Ridgebacks enjoy being close with family members.

Given a choice, he prefers to associate with other Ridgebacks rather than a dog of another breed. Despite his courage and ability, the Rhodesian Ridgeback is not a fighter, and will only quarrel if pushed into it. As a guardian, his instinct is strong but not apparent unless there is good cause. He makes no noisy show of his job; a look, a firm stance and a menacing growl that chills to the bone is usually more than sufficient. Thankfully he is an excellent judge of who is friendly and who is not, and rarely will his tougher side be shown.

chapter 2

The Rhodesian Ridgeback's Ancestry

Although still a relatively new breed in terms of standardization, the forebears of today's Rhodesian Ridgeback can be traced with certainty back to an account written in 1719. And evidence of drop-eared dogs bearing ridges exists in Egyptian drawings dating prior to 3000 B.C.,

suggesting that ridged dogs have been known to man perhaps since the beginning of civilization and before.

While its origins are most certainly ancient, the history of the development of the ridged hound remains largely speculation. The native African tribes did not keep breeding records of their dogs, no matter how integral to survival they were. So the Ridgeback's traceable history essentially begins with the exploration of Africa, although the dog's ancestors had no doubt been there for centuries before. For our purpose, a good starting point will be the arrival of Europeans

17

and their subsequent influence on the Ridgeback's ancestors.

The Ridgeback in Africa

To understand the Rhodesian Ridgeback, you must first know the conditions that necessitated the formation of this unique, versatile breed. Much of eighteenth century Africa was hostile territory. Naturally, dogs became integral players in the everyday struggle for existence, and a dog's responsibility to his master was formidable. Dogs were expected to protect the master and his family from dangerous predators and an often-unfriendly native element. They were on guard during the night to keep these same dangers away from the compound, livestock and possessions of the family. For reasons of food, protection and sport the dog also helped his master hunt all manner of creatures, most of which were very willing and eminently capable of fighting back. If game and supplies were scarce, the dogs were required to procure their own sustenance as well. A dog was "on duty" 24 hours a day, 365 days a year. To survive in a savage land, a dog needed the keenest of senses, infallible survival instinct and a hardy constitution. Death for both man and beast was commonplace and often brutal. In his authoritative work, *The Definitive Rhodesian Ridgeback,* David Helgesen writes:

> At no point in the history of the domestication of dogs have they been asked to perform more dangerous tasks under more hazardous natural conditions than they were on the southern African plateau. These ancestors of the modern Ridgeback were tough, tough, tough—or they did not survive. Not only did they have to survive the normal diseases such as distemper and occasionally rabies. They had to survive the most varied and deadly array of flora and fauna ever faced by dogs (p. 37).

Dogs were routinely lost to a formidable variety of dangerous predators, from lions to poisonous snakes. Additionally, tsetse flies, ticks and fleas carried deadly diseases and caused open sores and infection to the dogs. And the country itself was less than gentle. The terrain varied from scorching deserts to low-lying humid plains to open forested areas, each with their own natural hazards. Africa was a continual succession of thorns, burrs, hard-packed rock and earth, and even mud holes to the depth of a man's waist, all of which caused misery for the people and dogs who lived there. Survival of the fittest was not just a theory for the early European settlers in Africa; it was a way of life. This was the harsh and unrelenting wilderness that produced the indomitable guardian and hunter known to us today as the Rhodesian Ridgeback.

The Rhodesian's natural habitat was an unforgiving wilderness.

The Dog's Introduction to Europeans

The single most important ancestor of the modern Ridgeback is the half-wild Khoikhoi dog associated with the tribe of people bearing the same name (also called Hottentots by the Dutch). These were first noticed by European settlers near Cape Town in what is now South Africa, the first settlement being established there by the Dutch in 1652. This dog was greatly admired by the settlers (Afrikaners) for several distinctive traits: faithfulness and ferocity in guarding people and possessions, and speed, cunning and courage in

*The Mastiff is
one of many
types of dogs
that contributed
to the heritage
of today's
Rhodesian
Ridgeback.*

the hunt. Additionally, this dog showed the unique ridge of hair that stood up along the spine and ran against the lie of the rest of the coat, a mark that easily distinguished the Khoikhoi from other native dogs.

The settlers quickly discovered that the European dogs they brought with them were rarely able to withstand the rigors of Africa. Although they wished to keep some of the characteristics from the breeds of their homelands, they knew they needed a hardier animal capable of dealing with the fearsome predators and natural hazards they found in this harsh land. Lions, leopards, baboons, hyenas, jackals, poisonous snakes and insects all were significant threats to humans and livestock in the 1700s; dangers they had never before encountered. Nor did the pure European breeds have the correct combination of courage, temperament, hunting prowess, strength and gritty constitution to combat these threats. Bred for centuries to hunt much less formidable prey under far gentler conditions, the imported dogs were at a distinct disadvantage. They did not have the necessary instincts, nor were they able to adapt. It didn't take long for the Afrikaners to interbreed the Khoikhoi dog with their imported European dogs. These included both scenthounds and sighthounds of varying sizes and coat textures, Bulldogs, terriers, Mastiff types and sporting dogs. Interestingly, the unique ridge which the Khoikhoi dog passed on to many offspring of these crosses came to be seen as a special mark of courage and symbolized the most desirable traits of that indigenous breed to the Afrikaners. Dogs marked with the ridge became highly prized.

European missionaries were the first Caucasians to push toward the interior of Africa, followed closely by the big-game hunters beginning in the late 1840s to early 1850s. Both groups brought the dogs with them necessary to their lives and livelihoods, and over time ridged dogs migrated to all portions of the African continent alongside the brave adventurers who challenged the land.

THE "FIRST" RIDGEBACKS

How the inheritance of those ridged crossbred dogs formed the beginnings of a new breed is a fascinating tale of two men, one a missionary, the other a big-game hunter. In the year 1879, as closely as can be determined, the Reverend Charles Helm obtained in his travels two bitches for his use at the Hope Fountain Mission Station in Bulawayo (Rhodesia). Whether it was coincidence or fate, also in 1879 the Reverend Helm presided over the marriage of one Cornelius van Rooyen. We know that van Rooyen and Helm established a friendly relationship that lasted their entire lives. It is documented that at an early point in their friendship at least one of the Helm bitches was bred to a dog called "Flam" (translation: Flame) belonging to van Rooyen. The dates are unclear, but the result of this breeding was a litter of puppies with red coats, bobbed tails and ridged backs, the latter being a trait which Cornelius van Rooyen had not previously encountered in his own animals. We know that van Rooyen himself credits the Helm dogs with introducing the ridge

WHERE DID DOGS COME FROM?

It can be argued that dogs were right there at the side of the first Homo sapiens. As soon as human beings began to document their existence, the dog was among their drawings and inscriptions. Dogs were not just friends, they served a purpose: There were dogs to hunt birds, pull sleds, herd sheep, burrow after rats—even sit in laps! What your dog was originally bred to do influences the way he behaves. The American Kennel Club recognizes over 140 breeds, and there are hundreds more distinct breeds around the world. To make sense of the breeds, they are grouped according to their size or function. The AKC has seven groups:

1. Sporting   5. Terriers
2. Working   6. Toys
3. Herding   7. Non Sporting
4. Hounds

Can you name a breed from each group? Here's some help: (1) Golden Retriever; (2) Doberman Pinscher; (3) Collie; (4) Beagle; (5) Scottish Terrier; (6) Maltese; and (7) Dalmatian. All modern domestic dogs (*Canis familiaris*) are related, however different they may look, and are all descended from *Canis lupus*, the gray wolf.

into his pack of hunting dogs. Over the years, numerous breedings between the dogs owned by van Rooyen and Helm would take place.

For the next 35 years, Cornelius van Rooyen bred and developed a pack of ridged dogs that he used with great success on all manner of game. Most of his life was spent in leading hunting expeditions, and later in obtaining live animals that were ultimately sold to zoos around the world. In the course of that lifetime, he developed a new dog breed that became famous for its intelligence, speed and agility, endurance and hunting ability under the most adverse conditions. Van Rooyen's dogs were used to track game, flush it from cover and into the open and then hold it at bay until the hunters arrived for the kill or capture. This process could take a few minutes or many hours, depending upon the prey and the terrain. The dogs were asked to handle every sort of creature from wild fowl to many of Africa's most dangerous predators. Most notably, van Rooyen's dogs earned a reputation for their courage and skill in keeping lions at bay. Most dogs would not approach a lion under any circumstances, but van Rooyen's ridged pack consistently did so with great success. Thus a "Lion Dog" obtained from van Rooyen's stock was a valuable animal. The Ridgeback is still said to be the only breed capable of coming face-to-face with the African lion and surviving.

> **FAMOUS RHODESIAN RIDGEBACK OWNERS**
>
> Terry Anderson
>
> Errol Flynn
>
> Bob Guccione
>
> Wynonna Judd
>
> Carl Lewis
>
> Greg Louganis
>
> Patrick Swayze

Major Tom Hawley, a renowned Rhodesian Ridgeback breeder, judge and historian, has seen Ridgebacks at work in their homeland for many years. In his *The Rhodesian Ridgeback, The Origin, History and Standard,* he describes a typical encounter between a lion and a Ridgeback:

> The Ridgeback, singly or in a pack, will silently track the lion to its lair and only on discovery of its quarry will it give tongue; tantalising, feinting, darting in and out, just beyond the reach of those fearful slashing claws, with the nonchalance of a matador; harassing and wearing it down until that

majestic creature, bewildered by such elusive impudence and weary of trying to shake off its tenacious nuisance, presents a sitting target of injured majesty.

Such a performance postulates courage of a special kind, extraordinary agility and an uncanny discretion (p. 30).

Cornelius van Rooyen died in 1915, and so did not live to see the end result of his years of breeding and training his famous hunting dogs. As closely intertwined as their lives had been, it is a curious twist of fate that his lifelong friend and the man who was responsible for putting ridges on his dogs, the Reverend Charles Helm, died just sixteen days before van Rooyen.

The Ridgeback Is Recognized

In 1922, a fancier, F. R. Barnes, called a general meeting open to all owners of the ridged-back "Lion Dogs" to be held during the Bulawayo Kennel Club show. The purpose of that meeting was to create a written Standard, with the goal of eventual recognition by the South African Kennel Union as a distinct breed. By all accounts it was a motley assortment of dogs and owners present on that important day, but from that gathering the foundation of the breed as we know it today was established. By picking and choosing the most desirable traits of the dogs present, a breed Standard was created at that meeting. That original Standard, with very few modifications, has served as the blueprint of the perfect Ridgeback ever since.

The inception of the Rhodesian Ridgeback Standard is so recent that photographs exist of some of the earliest dogs from which the breed originated. These are a fascinating and invaluable record of the development of this remarkable hunting dog.

Ridgebacks in the U.S.

The first recorded imports of Ridgebacks to the United States occurred in the late 1940s. Almost from the day their paws first touched this country, a concerted effort was made to advance the breed. By 1955, a small group of dedicated breeder/fanciers had won American Kennel Club (AKC) recognition for the Rhodesian Ridgeback, and the Ridgeback's popularity has climbed slowly but steadily ever since. While still something of a secret to the general public, nonetheless the Ridgeback acquires new fans every day. Most people who have shared their lives with a Rhodesian Ridgeback find they cannot be without at least one, and their love for the breed is steadfast forever after.

BEST of BREED
(Variety)

Compared with many other breeds, the Ridgeback is a relatively "new" dog. This photo depicts a winning dog from the late 1960s.

THE HERITAGE CONTINUES

Three-quarters of a century is often no more time than the life span of a single person, and yet in this period the Ridgeback has become popular in countries all around the globe. Although his archenemy, the African lion, is never seen on the North American continent outside captivity, the Ridgeback's instincts and abilities survive and are put to excellent use in many other capacities. All over this continent, Ridgebacks have been used to hunt bear and bobcat, deer and wild boar, to control coyotes on large ranches and safeguard livestock from the cougar.

In other countries outside Africa, their hunting talents have been successfully utilized on a large number of different species indigenous to those areas. Their versatility in handling any type of game or terrain is well proven. Additionally, their extraordinary capabilities as guard dog are effectively used on large estates and in many homes as well.

I sold a puppy to the owners of a goat and sheep farm in northern California some years ago. When this dog was about 4 years old, the owners called me with an amazing story. Cougars were common in their area, and there had been substantial losses of livestock and even some human deaths from the cats. As a protected species, cougars could not be killed unless they were endangering lives. One night, while the household was sleeping, the three Ridgebacks became agitated, and commands to "be quiet" had minimal effect. When morning came and the dogs were let out of the house,

The regal Ridgeback continues to serve as a hunter and guard dog.

the male immediately streaked off towards the lower sheep pasture, where the owners heard the sounds of a confrontation with a cougar.

The two female Ridgebacks ran to aid the dog. By the time the owners arrived the cougar had beaten a hasty retreat, and the three Ridgebacks were standing guard over the carcass of a dead sheep, which the cougar had apparently been trying to drag over the pasture fence. With no training and no previous contact with these dangerous cats, the Ridgebacks knew instinctively what to do. None of the dogs had received even a scratch. By paying attention to the dogs' warning signals and acting promptly, the owners sustained only minimal losses from the cougars in their vicinity since that time.

Today, although the majority of Rhodesian Ridgebacks never come in contact with anything more dangerous than the ordinary housecat, they continue to serve and protect their people with the same unfailing loyalty their ancestors exhibited in the African bush.

chapter 3

The **World**
According to the
Rhodesian Ridgeback

Rhodesian Ridgebacks tend to view the world as their oyster. Much like the majestic lion they became famous for hunting, they walk through life with awe-inspiring confidence and grace. Each day brings new adventures that are happily anticipated, and enjoyed to the fullest. Ridgebacks, like all dogs, have an amazing capacity to appreciate the simple things life has to offer.

The breathtakingly powerful Rhodesian Ridgeback adds a dignified, beautiful presence to the lives he touches. But an owner needs to be aware that a Ridgeback is every bit as demanding as he is giving. He insists on respect, fair play and on having his feeding, exercise and intellectual needs met, and woe to the human who does not live up to his standards!

Hounds are famous (or infamous) for their stubborn, independent natures. Ridgebacks are no exception, although that stubborn streak is tempered with keen intelligence and a highly developed sense of humor. A Ridgeback can be both challenging and exhilarating to live with, but never will he be boring!

A Family Dog

If the world is his oyster, then a Ridgeback's human family is the pearl in its center. Ridgebacks insist on making themselves very much a part of the family. They are companionable and inquisitive by nature, and like to be in close proximity to their people as

Ridgebacks bond closely with their special person.

much as possible. A Ridgeback is usually found sitting or lying very near, or even on top of, the feet of one of his family members. Given the slightest opportunity and no encouragement whatsoever, a Ridgeback will usually end up sprawled across somebody's lap. An outing with the family, a walk in the park or a good snuggle with a special person are all events that bring great joy to this valiant fellow.

Rhodesian Ridgebacks are extremely loyal one-person dogs. As a puppy, a Ridgeback chooses "his" person, and attaches himself to that person for life. He will love the other members of the family, but his first loyalty will be firm. If parted from his owner, a Ridgeback will grieve long and hard. He can learn to love a new owner, but that first bond will never be forgotten.

Convinced that he is second in command only to his special person, a Ridgeback is certain to keep on top of all the activity in the household. No package is left uninspected, no dinner menu unapproved, no children's game or telephone conversation unsupervised.

While not intrusive, a Ridgeback can always be found wherever the action is. To isolate a Ridgeback away from the family is cruel. A bored or unhappy Ridgeback left to his own devices can become a destructive nuisance. Ridgebacks are rather industrious and will use their energy and intellect to think up various entertainments for themselves. While generally not inclined to dig, a Ridgeback can easily create large catacombs in your yard if left alone outside too much of the time. His voice is impressive (some even roar), and should he choose to vocally express his displeasure at being isolated from his human family, the neighbors would surely have every right to complain.

Rhodesian Ridgebacks are extremely athletic and strong-willed and may turn their time and energy into finding escape routes, which can be dangerous to their welfare. In short, there is no point in owning a Ridgeback if he is not considered a true member of the family with the same need for attention, activity and companionship as any of his human counterparts.

CHARACTERISTICS OF THE RHODESIAN RIDGEBACK

Loyal

Strong

Gentle

Comical

Independent

Active

Playful

Reserved with strangers

RIDGEBACKS AND CHILDREN

Rhodesian Ridgebacks have a special relationship with children. They are gentle, protective and adoring of them. Both children and Ridgebacks need to be taught how to respect each other and interact nicely, or a loving relationship can not happen, but once the bond is forged it will never be broken. Even Ridgebacks who have not been raised with children enjoy their attention, and are especially interested in babies and toddlers.

If a Ridgeback grows tired of a child's games or wants to be left alone, he will simply remove himself from the room. Bitches tend to be the self-appointed guardians of little ones. They will station themselves several feet away from a sleeping baby and stand guard for hours, not relieving themselves from duty until the baby awakens or is moved. Male Ridgebacks tend to like the more active attention of slightly older children. A young, energetic dog can unintentionally topple a small child, and needs to be taught to control his size and strength, but this is generally accomplished with a natural ease. Too many times to count I have seen a huge male Ridgeback patiently lying on his bed wagging his tail, while a young child hugs, kisses, climbs on top of him and whispers secrets in his ear. When visitors asked about the Ridgeback this little girl would proudly announce "That's Congo, he's my puppy."

RIDGEBACKS AND OTHER PETS

Adult Ridgebacks accept other dogs and pets, and fit easily into multiple-animal households. In suburban and rural areas they are popular barn and stable dogs because of their size and ability to keep up with a horse while enjoying the exercise, and because of their nonaggressive nature with other domestic animals. Ridgebacks will not fight unless given no other choice. All in all, they are amiable, gregarious and unobtrusive unless compelled to be otherwise.

The exuberance of kids and the patience of Ridgebacks make them a perfect match!

The Canine Comic

The Rhodesian Ridgeback's sense of humor is sheer delight. They love nothing better than a good laugh, often at the expense of the foolish humans who inhabit their domain. Interestingly enough, the color of a Ridgeback's nose can direct his expression of humor. The black-nosed dogs most often enjoy a laugh at someone else's expense, be it a person or another pet in the household. They enjoy helping their people learn about the humor in everyday life. One of my black-nosed girls loved nothing better than to "pull a fast one" on the unsuspecting. One day I observed her stalking my husband, who was working in the yard. Belly to the ground, she would creep up silently behind her unsuspecting victim and patiently wait for the perfect moment. When he bent over to pick up a tool, she sprang into action. Two long bounds and a flying leap through the air saw both of her front paws planted firmly on his rear. While her "prey" pitched face-first into the ground, a very happy Ridgeback bounced out of sight wearing a big grin.

The typical Ridgeback will go out of his way to get a smile.

Another black-nosed dog thoroughly enjoyed tormenting the family cat, however not in the usual dog-chases-cat manner. Upon cornering the cat, he would scoop her up in his mouth and parade her around the house. The cat would be kicking and squirming, the Ridgeback prancing and grinning. When her feline pride had been thoroughly insulted, he would deposit her on the floor, none the worse for the wear, other than the added injury of having to groom the dog drool from her coat.

In contrast, the liver-nosed dogs are more apt to turn humor on themselves to entertain their family. They are more exuberantly clownish. My liver-nosed bitch, always sensitive to my mood, would take it upon herself to cheer me up if she sensed that I was feeling blue. Her usual method was to chase her tail in circles at high speed until she was in danger of falling over. At which point she would stop, check to see if I was smiling yet and begin the chase again in the opposite direction. It always worked.

One particularly endearing trait of nearly all Ridgebacks is their special device for attracting attention.

They lie on their side on the ground and place their paws behind their ears. Then the paws are drawn down the length of the face to the nose with the tail thumping, while they peek at their person out of the corner of an eye. This maneuver is repeated until the desired results are obtained, that is, until someone gives them the attention they seek. Interestingly enough, the only other breed I have ever seen use this same gesture is the Basenji, another African breed.

Keep Your Dog Entertained, Too!

When not involving themselves in family matters, Ridgebacks will devise their own amusements, which may not be suitable to their surroundings. They should be provided with appropriate toys and given direction as to what is acceptable.

Ridgebacks are champion chewers and must be supplied with the most durable and indestructible toys available. Never allow a Ridgeback to chew on household items, as he will inevitably destroy them and may ingest something very harmful in the process. Old socks and shoes should never be used as toys, for

All dogs, especially puppies, need to chew. If you want your possessions left intact, toys for chewing are a must!

example. There are several very durable chew toys on the market that are safe for your Ridgeback, and they are well worth the investment. Once I returned home from running a quick errand and found my 7-year-old in the middle of the floor chewing on a large flashlight! She had apparently rooted around in the kitchen cupboards for something to occupy her time. Upon my arrival, she merely smiled and thumped her tail, well-pleased with having amused herself in my absence.

Intelligence and Instinct

The Rhodesian Ridgeback is one of the most intelligent of all dogs. Your Ridgeback is very quick to learn what you expect of him, and while he wants to please you, his stubborn streak sometimes gets in the way. Do not expect instant or unfailing obedience! But remember that this independence is a natural result of what a Ridgeback was bred to do. He was bred to track and bay quarry, and to guard against dangerous enemies—both animal and human. To do so, he had to think for himself. His role in life demanded high intelligence, a strong instinct for survival and the ability to work without guidance from his master, always questioning the world around him and deciding for himself the best way of coping. His keen senses often saved the lives of his people, who would unknowingly find themselves in dangerous situations. So it should be no surprise that perfect obedience does not come easily to a Ridgeback; he is always questioning whether or not you know what you are about!

TRAINING THE PET RIDGEBACK

Start training sessions when your dog is a pup—you'll be surprised at how quickly a puppy catches on.

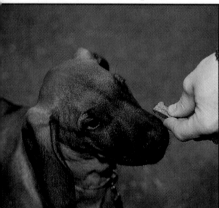

Nonetheless, a dog with the size and power of a Rhodesian Ridgeback must be taught basic manners and obedience commands from an early age. All Ridgebacks are capable of learning the skills needed to be a pleasurable companion. They are intelligent, intuitive and responsive to pleasing you. I suggest beginning with a puppy kindergarten or socialization class when your puppy is about 4 months of age, and following this up with a second class to teach further basic obedience exercises, which should be started no older than 8 months of age. If he masters in these two courses the basic obedience commands, your Ridgeback will never forget them, and will be your treasured companion for his entire lifetime. By training your dog as a puppy, you will encourage his belief that you, as a human, are bigger, stronger and wiser than your dog. (Note, however, that your Ridgeback will rather quickly surmise that he is far the wiser, and will not be fooled in this respect for very long!) Additionally, if you establish good control of your puppy before he reaches adolescence, when hormones are raging and he is acting like a rebellious teenager, that phase of the puppy experience will be easier to manage.

If you are fortunate enough to adopt an older Ridgeback, obedience classes are an excellent way to form a lasting bond with your new pet. Even if a dog has had training in the past, a refresher course will acquaint him with your desires and style of leadership. Respect and trust between dog and owner are quickly learned in a good obedience class.

To demand more of a Ridgeback than he feels is proper invites creative disobedience. The duty to obey the master sometimes battles for control with this breed's independent nature. If you request a response from your Ridgeback that he finds distasteful, boring or an unnecessary waste of time, creative thinking on his part usually offers an interesting solution, although rarely a desired one.

When training one of my girls for competitive obedience, it quickly became clear that she found the broad jump exercise thoroughly stupid. There was no need to jump that thing when she could simply avoid it altogether! After several frustrating weeks of butting heads, my Ridgeback arrived at her version of a compromise. Upon being placed in position to perform the broad jump she would crease back her ears, drop her head, squint her eyes and let the whole world know she was thoroughly disgusted. At my signal, she would perform the broad jump flawlessly—once. One perfect

Training reinforces respect and trust between you and your Ridgeback.

broad jump. I was never able to coax her to do more than one in a training session; any efforts at a repeat performance only led to imaginative ways of avoiding the exercise entirely. Never have I found an individual from another dog breed that thinks and reasons as intelligently as does a Rhodesian Ridgeback.

ACCENTUATE THE POSITIVE

Keen intellect is accompanied by an incredible memory. Good or bad, friend or foe, a Ridgeback never forgets. Harsh treatment always leaves a poor impression with a Ridgeback. Being very intelligent and intuitive, your Ridgeback knows what you are feeling; he can read your moods with ease.

Physical punishment is always due to an owner's loss of control rather than any need for it by the Ridgeback. He clearly understands your tone of voice and body language, and your verbal displeasure is punishment enough for any transgression. Large dogs do not need harsher treatment than their smaller counterparts. In fact, no dog requires physical punishment, regardless of his size. Ridgebacks are gentle and easily coaxed into good behavior with love and praise. When training your Ridgeback, remember that harsh collar corrections only teach your dog that obedience is distasteful and to be avoided; praise and positive reinforcement is the only sure way to achieve success.

NATURALLY NEAT!

The Ridgeback's coat is naturally short, glossy and odor-free, and there is minimal shedding, making him an ideal house dog from the neatness perspective. Ridgebacks are instinctively clean and a puppy can be housetrained in just a few days. They are dry-mouthed, and do not ordinarily drool (except perhaps in anticipation of an impending meal). In short, Rhodesian Ridgebacks are nearly perfect house pets.

The Ridgeback's Development

As a large breed, Rhodesian Ridgebacks are very slow to mature, both physically and mentally. As they grow from puppies to adults, they go through several growth phases, which all have endearing traits as well as developmental setbacks and problems.

PUPPYHOOD

A baby puppy is sweet, happy, inquisitive and outgoing. His curiosity often gets him into mischief, but it is all done in innocence. It is, therefore, easy to spoil the pup because of the "cuteness factor"; you just can't help it. However this is the most important developmental period in a Ridgeback's life, and he needs a great deal of gentle correction and guidance. Housetraining, proper socialization, basic obedience and dominance issues are all occurring during the period from birth until about 8 months of age, and each must be dealt with correctly and firmly in order to develop a happy, confident, enjoyable adult.

The proper way to interact with both people and other dogs is the core of all of these issues, which is why it seems gentle guidance is required practically every moment! Thankfully, puppies absorb lessons like a sponge absorbs water and learn the necessary skills quickly; they just need lots of practice and reinforcement after that. It is a huge responsibility to mold a young dog into a happy, confident adult animal; one which consumes large amounts of your time and atten-

Gentle interaction with people of all ages sets the stage for a puppy to grow into an accepting, confident adult.

tion but which rewards you with many years of joy that make it all worthwhile.

Socialization and obedience classes are instrumental in helping to develop your Ridgeback puppy's fullest potential, as is the advice of his breeder, who has done this all before. Chapter 8 of this book gives you excellent basic training information you will find invaluable as you work with your young Ridgeback.

The early puppy stage is also a time of tremendous physical growth and development, with many changes.

Your puppy will be in the teething stage this entire time, so appropriate chew toys and the correct reinforcing of rules regarding chewing are very important. If you find your pup chewing on something he should not be, take the object away and tell him "no" in a calm, firm voice. Then offer your pup an acceptable puppy toy in its place. Most pups accept the trade quite readily, and your goal is accomplished with a minimum of fuss or upset.

In just eight months your puppy will grow from a weight of approximately 12 or 15 pounds to a range of from 50 to 65 pounds! Growth stages are very apparent, with puppies shifting in and out between gawky and beautiful and goofy stages of growth, both mentally and physically. These different stages can last as little as a week or as long as a couple of months. Your bitch puppy may have a pointed backskull or be higher in the hips than at the shoulders. She may have long, slender legs and a tail to match or she may suddenly grow large, unfeminine knuckles and feet. Your male Ridgeback puppy may be clumsy and uncoordinated one day, graceful and balanced the next. His head and feet may look too large for his body, or too small. Your pup may act like a mature, responsible adult one moment but almost immediately revert to baby puppy antics! Just remember that all the growth and changes that occur are harder on your puppy than they are on you; after all, he is the one trying to make sense of the world.

Ridgebacks waste no time growing up. This "little" dog is only 3 months old.

TEEN TIME

Somewhere around 8 months of age, your Ridgeback puppy will enter his adolescent period. Hormones begin to play a large factor in your puppy's behavior and attitude at this time. If you have not already done so, this is the time to have your puppy spayed or neutered (see Chapter 7 for the health benefits of spaying/neutering). Your Ridgeback puppy will begin to act like a 15-year-old teenager, questioning your authority, and sometimes acting openly rebellious.

While remaining sweet and loving, the adolescent Ridgeback can be expected to test the limits you have previously set for him. With patient, gentle corrections and reminders of who is truly in charge, you will weather this period of your pup's development without incident. Some retraining may be required, and some established privileges may have to be temporarily revoked to ensure your Ridgeback's safety. By this time your pup is already quite large, so it may be hard to remember that he is still just a puppy. He will be typically exuberant, rambunctious and energetic. This phase does not last long, and soon your pup will begin to act more mature; normally by no later than 16 months of age.

Adult Dogs

The adult Ridgeback is an extraordinarily enjoyable companion. This dog is happy to lie contentedly in the midst of family activity and simply enjoy being part of the life around him. Adult Ridgebacks are quiet, and are not inclined to bark unnecessarily. They are aware of all that goes on around them but feel no need to comment unless they perceive a threat.

Senior Citizens

Ridgebacks are relatively healthy and, for a large breed, long-lived; the average life span ranges between ten and twelve years. As your Ridgeback matures from an adult in the prime of life into a senior citizen, subtle changes begin to take place. Your older Ridgeback may be content to sleep longer, and more soundly. He may not run and play as hard as he once did. The older Ridgeback mellows with age and becomes less concerned with dominance and status, being very secure in his position in family hierarchy. As the dog's face slowly turns from dark to gray to pure white, the older Ridgeback exhibits a wisdom, grace and balance of spirit that has its own special beauty.

A senior Ridgeback may become fussy and demanding and more easily upset by changes in routine and surroundings. He will probably be less able to withstand extremes of temperature. Joints and muscles may ache, and your senior may need a few special considerations because of health concerns. The senior will probably feel free to flaunt the rules with impunity, understanding that no scolding erases the joy of sleeping on the forbidden sofa, and secure in the knowledge that you will not punish him anyway. The senior Ridgeback has earned the right to make his own rules. Indeed, the special little pleasures and idiosyncrasies of the elderly Ridgeback make him all the more dear.

As a Ridgeback ages, he's likely to be most concerned about a soft spot on the couch.

For more on the care requirements of the older Ridgeback, please see Chapter 7, "Keeping Your Rhodesian Ridgeback Healthy."

The Ridgeback as Protector

An uncanny intuition about who is friend or foe is a nearly legendary trait of the adult Ridgeback. Ridgebacks quietly accept newcomers that they sense are friendly but will keep a close eye on those they distrust. Your Ridgeback may act standoffish towards new people for the first few minutes after meeting them. He will watch, smell and intuit the person before making up his mind whether or not the visitor is acceptable. If the guest passes muster, your Ridgeback will gladly accept petting and attention, and a friendship will be formed. If the dog dislikes the visitor, he will clearly snub all friendly overtures, and may keep a watchful eye on the unwelcome guest for as long as that person remains in your Ridgeback's territory.

If you wish your Ridgeback to have protective instincts towards your family and property, do not fear that training him to behave properly around people will subdue his natural guarding abilities. Many Ridgebacks are so easygoing and gentle that their owners never see any signs of protectiveness. Your dog is an incredibly astute judge of character, and should the need arise, he will be there to do his job, as his ancestors have always done.

My first male Ridgeback was one such sweet, gentle dog who loved everyone he encountered. I had *never* heard this dog growl or show the protective side of his nature until one day when he was 3 years old. A woman appeared at my door claiming to be a real estate agent sent to look over the property. Upon her stepping into the house, my dog growled long and deep and rushed to the front of his crate with hackles raised. He was very upset by the presence of this woman in his territory, and as it later turned out, he was right. This woman had never been sent to evaluate the property, and she had lied her way into my home for purposes I don't even like to think about! I have since learned to trust my dogs absolutely if they take offense to anyone. Just as he never forgets a friend, neither does the Ridgeback forget or forgive those he considers his enemies. His memory and character judgment are infallible.

Although generally gentle, Ridgebacks will protect their family should the need arise.

Exercise Needs

Ridgebacks are champion sleepers and enjoy a good snooze in the sun, or next to the fireplace in winter. But pick up a collar and leash, and in an instant your happy, eager, energetic friend will be at your side ready to join you in an outing!

A Rhodesian Ridgeback does need plentiful exercise. To develop correct muscles and proper movement, and to keep him mentally and physically fit, he will need brisk walks on a lead, and a safe, enclosed place to run. Ridgebacks love to run, and your hound at full extension is a truly awesome sight.

He must be given a safe place to run at full speed at least twice a week. If your yard is not large enough for your pet to really stretch out in, search out large parks, high school or college playing fields or other similar locations that are both fenced and secure. Be very certain to give all public areas the respect they deserve, and clean up after your pet. Also be aware that a large dog running loose can intimidate many people, and they will not know that your Ridgeback is friendly. Use any public area at a time when it will be less heavily frequented, and be sure to obey any posted leash laws.

Walks are not the only activity your Ridgeback will enjoy. Hiking, camping and backpacking are favorites. Ridgebacks love the exercise they get from bicycling or rollerblading with you. Visiting with your well-trained pet is a pleasure for him as well as for you. And there are many, many organized activities to become involved in as well.

Ridgebacks can excel at Agility trials. The fast pace, physical demands and independent thinking required of a dog in Agility is perfectly suited to the Ridgeback's instincts. There are Lure Coursing trials and race meets on straight or oval tracks to attend. Therapy

A DOG'S SENSES

Sight: With their eyes located farther apart than ours, dogs can detect movement at a greater distance than we can, but they can't see as well up close. They can also see better in less light, but can't distinguish many colors.

Sound: Dogs can hear about four times better than we can, and they can hear high-pitched sounds especially well. Their ancestors, the wolves, howled to let other wolves know where they were; our dogs do the same, but they have a wider range of vocalizations, including barks, whimpers, moans and whines.

Smell: A dog's nose is his greatest sensory organ. His sense of smell is so great he can follow a trail that's weeks old, detect odors diluted to one-millionth the concentration we'd need to notice them and even sniff out a person under water!

Taste: Dogs have fewer taste buds than we do, so they're likelier to try anything—and usually do, which is why it's especially important for their owners to monitor their food intake. Dogs are omnivores, which means they eat meat as well as vegetable matter like grasses and weeds.

Touch: Dogs are social animals and love to be petted, groomed and played with.

work visiting hospitals and nursing homes requires some specialized training and testing for certification but is highly rewarding for both you and your Ridgeback. You can train your Ridgeback to become a fine Tracking dog and compete in AKC Tracking tests. A few Ridgebacks have shown herding capabilities, or have been trained as gun dogs.

In short, there is very little that a Ridgeback cannot accomplish with encouragement and training. As long as you approach an activity with an attitude of fun and companionship (not work and forced obedience), your Ridgeback is game for anything!

One of the few things Rhodesian Ridgebacks do not enjoy is water. Most Ridgebacks do not care to swim, probably because they are not very good at it. A Ridgeback's substantial bone and muscle translates to weight. This, combined with a low percentage of body fat in proportion to size and muscle mass, renders him not particularly buoyant in the water. In short, a Ridgeback tends to sink rather than float, and swimming is hard work.

Lure Coursing events are a favorite of Ridgebacks. These trials are a great opportunity to stretch those legs.

THE IMPORTANCE OF CONTAINMENT

A Ridgeback should never be let loose in an unfenced area. His keen eyes and nose will put him on the trail of a cat, squirrel or other interesting scent. If a Ridgeback is enticed out of his own yard, he will not stop at property lines or roads. He will continue the chase with no thought of anything else, and could easily become lost or hurt. You will need to have a securely enclosed yard, with your fence being at least 6 feet high. Ridgebacks are as good at jumping as they are bad at swimming and can clear tall obstacles easily. They are also intelligent enough to figure out how to open most gates and doors, and a bored dog will amuse himself by frustrating all your efforts to keep him safely enclosed.

Socializing Your Ridgeback

Rhodesian Ridgebacks need exercise for their minds as well as for their muscles. Even though my dogs have a large, safely fenced yard to play in, I take them all for regular walks around our neighborhood. Exposing your dog to a variety of different areas and situations gives him something to think about and helps to socialize him. The mental stimulation will help keep your dog alert to the world around him and contented within it. You will also meet many nice people on your walks who can not help but stop and ask about your Ridgeback. His powerful, dignified presence works like a magnet; he is a real "ice breaker."

The Canine Climate

Rhodesian Ridgebacks are supposed to be "tough" dogs, capable of withstanding the worst of weather

High, strong fencing is a necessity if your dog will be off-leash.

conditions. But to purposely expose your loyal pet to such extremes is cruel and dangerous. Your pet Ridgeback was not born or raised in Africa. During the hot summer months, he must have plenty of shade and fresh water if kept outdoors during the heat of the day.

I usually keep my dogs in the house during the hottest part of the day and let them out to play and exercise early in the morning and again at sundown when it is much cooler. If you feel too warm outdoors in the sun, so does your Ridgeback!

Winter is even harder on this sleek-coated breed. Ridgebacks hate the cold, and with good reason. Frostbite can occur quickly to ears, tails and feet if left unprotected in the cold, and since they have no heavy coat to keep out the chill, a Ridgeback's body temperature can also drop. Under no circumstances should the

Ridgeback living in a cold climate be made to remain outdoors during the winter. Older puppies or young adults may enjoy playing in the snow for awhile but should be brought indoors at the first sign of discomfort. Some Ridgebacks will wear a warm dog coat or sweater, but many appear to be embarrassed beyond words at being seen in such attire; their immense dignity simply does not permit it. The best rule of thumb is the same as for summer weather precautions: If you are cold outdoors without protection, so is your Ridgeback!

Just as they hate being cold, Ridgebacks also hate wet weather. If it is raining outside, they will stay in the house where it is dry, literally for days, rather than go outside for potty breaks! Some forceful urging is usually required to coax a Ridgeback outdoors in the rain.

Rhodesian Ridgeback Q&A

The questions you will get about your Ridgeback are amusing to those who know the breed, but very serious for the person doing

Meeting new people and seeing new things is important for your dog's social skills. Cruise the neighborhood with your Ridgeback!

the asking. Be prepared to answer patiently and honestly. The following are some of the questions most commonly heard from people meeting a Rhodesian Ridgeback for the first time:

- *His hair is standing up; will he bite me?*

Ridgebacks are not a commonly seen breed in many areas of the country, and people will have no idea what the ridge is and why it exists. Many will assume it is a sign of aggression. Once they have seen a Rhodesian Ridgeback and been informed about the ridge, a person rarely forgets the beautiful dog with the striking identification.

- *How do you make his hair go that way?*

Some people will believe that you have purposely cut or brushed your Ridgeback's hair into that funny pattern and will want to know why. Curious people are normally excited and amazed by the ridge once it is explained to them. The ridge is a naturally occurring feature that you can't mold or sculpt into place.

- *Where did the ridge come from?*

There isn't a good answer to this one, except that it has been passed down through the generations from the Ridgeback's wild Hottentot-owned ancestors. No attempt to identify the gene that produces the ridge has been made. The ridge is a mystery; and everybody loves a good mystery!

- *Is that one of those Razorbacks?*

Unfortunately, the word "razorback" is often used by the uninformed. A razorback is a wild pig found chiefly in the southeastern U.S. People certainly do not mean to offend anyone with this term, so take it as an opportunity to gently educate if you get asked this question.

- *They kill lions, don't they?*

Just getting within striking range of an African lion is impressive enough! Ridgebacks did not kill lions; they merely held them at bay for the hunter to deal with. Although Rhodesian Ridgebacks did in fact kill smaller cats like leopards, and other dangerous creatures like the fearsome adult baboon, their true talent was for survival, not foolhardy risk-taking.

More Information on Rhodesian Ridgebacks

NATIONAL BREED CLUB

Rhodesian Ridgeback Club of the United States (RRCUS)
Public Information
Deborah Hopper-Danford
2032 U.S. Hwy 401 S.
Louisburg, NC 27549-9801

Enclose check or money order for $2 for breed information or visit the Web site at http://www.rrcus.org.

BOOKS

Hawley, T. C. *The Rhodesian Ridgeback, The Origin, History and Standard.* Available from Natalie D. Carlton, 5630 N. Abington Road, Tucson, AZ 85743.

Helgesen, David H. *The Definitive Rhodesian Ridgeback,* 2nd ed. (revised). Available from D. H. Helgesen, Anglo-American Box 141, Pitts Meadows, British Columbia, V3Y 2E6, Canada.

Nicholson, Peter and Janet Parker. *The Complete Rhodesian Ridgeback.* New York: Howell Book House, 1991.

MAGAZINES

The Ridgeback, Rhodesian Ridgeback Club of the United States (RRCUS), 2032 U.S. Hwy 401 S., Louisburg, NC 27549-9801.

Official publication of the Rhodesian Ridgeback Club of the United States. Available only with paid membership to the RRCUS.

The Rhodesian Ridgeback Quarterly, Hoflin Publishing, 4401 Zephyr Street, Wheat Ridge, CO 80033-3299.

The AKC GAZETTE, The Official Journal for the Sport of Purebred Dogs, 5580 Centerview Drive, Raleigh, NC 27606-3390.

Official publication of the American Kennel Club; general interest with a quarterly column about Rhodesian Ridgebacks.

VIDEOS

American Kennel Club. *The Rhodesian Ridgeback,* #VVT416. American Kennel Club, Attn: Video Fulfillment, 5580 Centerview Drive, Suite 200, Raleigh, NC 27606.

Living
with a

part two

Rhodesian Ridgeback

chapter 4

Bringing Your
Rhodesian
Ridgeback
Home

When choosing a Rhodesian Ridgeback, a prospective owner must understand that the Ridgeback is a devoted one-person dog. To a Rhodesian Ridgeback, bonding to her owner is forever, and separation is a cruel reward for her incorruptible love. Ridgebacks live an average of 10 to 12 years, so if this is the breed you have chosen, be very certain of your commitment.

Where to Get Your Dog

Rhodesian Ridgebacks are rarely seen in pet shops, and newspaper ads for Ridgebacks are also few and far between. There are several ways to find a reputable, conscientious Rhodesian Ridgeback breeder. The best and easiest method is to contact the Rhodesian Ridgeback Club of the U.S. (RRCUS) (the address is given at the end of Chapter 3). The national breed club will provide you with information about Ridgebacks, including a nationwide list of RRCUS member-breeders who subscribe to the Club Code of Ethics. Many, but not all, reputable breeders belong to the RRCUS, and word of mouth is also a good method of contact.

EVALUATING A BREEDER

The conscientious breeder is not motivated by the prospect of making money. In fact, most good breeders are lucky not to lose money once the costs of breeding and raising a litter of puppies are considered. Very high prices are one indication that perhaps this breeder is not the one to buy from, as are exceptionally low prices (except for ridgeless puppies, which usually

are low-priced even from the best breeders). Not every breeder charges the same amount for their puppies, but comparison should show prices falling within a fairly narrow range. A reputable breeder will offer a written guarantee on the health of the puppy you are buying and will specify what action he will take should a problem occur.

By buying your puppy from a reputable breeder, you'll get a chance to view his facilities and to meet your new dog's dam.

Reputable breeders have proven the quality of their animals in competition, either at conformation shows or in performance events. Run, don't walk, away from the person who "knows" his dogs are quality, without being able to tell you why! Likewise, the breeder who "just breeds pets" or bred a litter because he "wanted one just like Shasha" is a poor choice. There are companion quality pups in every well-bred litter (just as there might be future champions), and this is what you should look for.

Adopting an Older Dog

If you are thinking of adopting an older Ridgeback, there is another avenue for you to utilize. The RRCUS has a nationwide rescue program that matches dogs needing homes with prospective adopters. Dogs available through the rescue program are animals the RRCUS has retrieved from shelters or abusive homes, abandoned or lost dogs whose owners can not be found or dogs turned in by owners who could no longer keep them. The rescue program evaluates the dogs and potential adopters and makes the best match possible.

Be Patient!

Whether you are looking for a puppy or for that special adult Ridgeback, the best advice is to be patient! Although the breed is growing in popularity, Ridgeback puppies or adults are not always available just when you want one. After speaking with several reputable breeders, choose the one you feel the most comfortable with and be willing to put down a deposit to hold a puppy from that breeder's next litter. In many cases, a breeder with an established reputation will have sold a number of pups from a particular litter before the puppies are even born.

Remember to use your head (as well as your heart) when choosing your puppy.

Pre-Arrival Purchases

There are a number of essentials you must have prior to bringing your Ridgeback home.

Your Dog's Special Place

The first and most important item to purchase is a dog crate. A dog crate is essential for the dog's emotional security, for your peace of mind and for the safety of the puppy and household. A crate reinforces the dog's natural denning instinct and is a secure, comfortable "bedroom" for your dog. It is a space that belongs wholly to her when she needs to get away from the world for awhile.

A crate is the single most important tool you will own when it comes to housetraining your puppy and for ensuring her safety when you can not be watching over her. As you can see, a dog crate is a must! The proper size crate for a Rhodesian Ridgeback is at least 26 inches tall for a bitch, or 28 inches tall for a dog. If you buy a crate of the proper height, the rest of the dimensions will be in the correct proportion.

A dog's crate is her own place to get away from it all.

There are two different crate styles: collapsible wire crates and fiber-glass airline-style crates. Either style is acceptable, although if you plan on doing any traveling with your pet, the airline-approved crate is the only type that can be used when flying your Ridgeback on a commercial airline.

Bedding

Your Ridgeback will grow into a large dog, with substantial bone. Like most members of her breed, she will be lean and muscular, without excess body fat. This means that your Ridgeback will need soft, supportive bedding in her crate and in any area of the house she may frequent. Without body fat to cushion

PUPPY ESSENTIALS

Your new puppy will need the following items:

food bowl

water bowl

collar

leash

ID tag

bed

crate

toys

grooming supplies

51

the pressure points, a Ridgeback can develop large callused areas where the hair is rubbed away and the skin becomes hard and black. These pressure sores are easily avoided by providing soft, well-cushioned bedding for your pet.

Puppies will usually chew on their beds as a matter of course, so be certain your pup has plenty of chew toys in her crate or bed area, and be prepared to repair or replace a bed or two until she outgrows this stage.

With their lean bodies, soft bedding is a must for Ridgebacks.

Other Essential Supplies

You will also need food and water dishes, grooming supplies (see Chapter 6 for a detailed list), appropriate chew toys and play toys, lead and collar with identification tags, training treats and a supply of the food she has been used to. You should already have chosen a veterinarian, who will be prepared for the arrival of your new pet as well.

FOOD

Ask the breeder before the big day arrives what brand of food your new pet has been eating, and be certain to lay in a supply of that food. If you choose to switch to a different brand later you may do so, but to avoid stomach upset and diarrhea, feed your Ridgeback the brand she is accustomed to for the first few weeks.

DOGGY DISHES

Food and water dishes are simple to choose. There are three appropriate basic types: stainless steel, plastic crock style and ceramic. The last is probably the least desirable because of its potential for breaking and harming your dog, but ceramic does have the advantage of being quite heavy and difficult for the dog to tip over or carry around.

It is better for a large dog to eat from a raised dish, as it helps to prevent choking and is easier on bones, joints and tendons. These are available from your local pet supply store or from mail-order pet supply catalogs.

TOYS

Toys for your Rhodesian Ridgeback must always be chosen with safety foremost in mind. Knowing that her jaws will be very strong and that she will chew on whatever is available, you must be careful to avoid any toy which can be broken up and ingested, or even swallowed whole. The safe ones are made of hard, dense rubber or nylon.

Fleece toys are a favorite of Ridgebacks, but be aware that such toys are easily shredded.

Toys are available in all kinds of interesting shapes and sizes, and some are particularly made with dental health in mind. Sterilized beef leg bones are great for Ridgebacks of all ages, and last forever. These are also available at most pet supply stores. But never give your Ridgeback other types of bones (chicken, pork or steak bones from your table), as these will easily splinter between her powerful jaws. When swallowed, the splinters can pierce the esophagus, stomach or intestines, which is a grave situation.

Fleece toys are appropriate for cuddling and tossing games, and Ridgebacks love them. But avoid toys that contain a squeaker device, as your pet will spend as long as it takes to destroy the toy and remove the squeaker. If swallowed, the squeaker can cause intestinal obstruction leading to emergency surgery and may even prove fatal. If your Ridgeback tends to destroy fleece toys, it is best to choose something else. The bones and toys made of soft cotton rope are great fun and are safe for playing tossing and pouncing games, and even for chewing needs.

STOCK UP ON TREATS

Treats for your new pet are one of the easiest items to buy. This is because a Ridgeback will eat anything! Hard biscuits are always a good choice for a treat because they will help to keep your pet's teeth clean. For more ideas on feeding special treats, refer to Chapter 5.

Especially intriguing for Ridgebacks are the toys that can be filled or stuffed with goodies. Not only can she chew on the toy, she will spend hours working on removing whatever food treat is inside. Peanut butter is a good toy stuffer (smear on the inside of a beef bone, for example), as are hard biscuit pieces, pieces of cheese or the tasty treats available in the pet food aisle at your local grocery store or supermarket. Even pieces of her regular dog food will work. When it comes to treats, Ridgebacks are not fussy!

Ridgebacks are not natural retrievers, and many have no interest whatsoever in playing with a ball. If your pet does enjoy balls, be sure to furnish only those that are large enough to not be inhaled or swallowed. Check carefully to see that the ball can not be ripped apart and the pieces swallowed. You may be very surprised at just what your pet's jaws are capable of, and the toys that you thought were indestructible, you will find in pieces on the floor! It is always better to err on the side of caution when choosing appropriate playthings for your Ridgeback.

Identification

A Ridgeback will outgrow several different collars before reaching full size, but it is very important that she have some form of identification at all times, in case she should become separated from you.

COLLARS AND TAGS

The easiest and most visible form of identification is a collar bearing tags that give your name, phone number and address. Rabies vaccination and dog license tags should also be worn. An identification tag is the first thing a person will look for if he finds a loose dog. All identification should be attached to a plain leather or nylon buckle style collar. Never leave a "choke" collar on your Ridgeback. These should be used only for training purposes. A Ridgeback wearing a choke collar can easily catch the collar on something in the house or yard and strangle to death within minutes. There is a specific reason why that type of collar is so named!

A tattoo is a great way to permanently identify your dog.

MODERN METHODS

Other identification methods include tattooing and microchipping. Both methods are permanent, infallible identification of your dog. I strongly advise that you choose to either tattoo or microchip your Rhodesian Ridgeback for several important reasons. Permanent methods prove conclusively your pet's identity and that she belongs to you. Most research laboratories that buy dogs for experimentation will notify the proper agency should they find they have obtained a dog that is tattooed or microchipped. This is invaluable protection for your pet.

Leashes

The style of leash, or lead, you choose is for the most part a matter of personal preference, but a few pointers are in order. The thinner the lead, the more comfortable it will feel in your hand. Leads are much stronger than they appear, and my favorite leads are no more than ½-inch wide.

Make sure that you buy a leash that has sufficient length for ease of walking with your pet. I have found that 5- or 6-foot leashes work best. The retractable leads are wonderful for exercise; however, I do not advise trying to train a puppy on this type of leash. Your Ridgeback needs to know how to walk nicely on a lead without dragging you down the sidewalk before being given the freedom of a retractable lead.

The most popular leashes are made of durable, lightweight materials. Pick one that is comfortable for you and your Ridgeback.

Select a Veterinarian

One final preparation should be made for your Ridgeback prior to her arrival, and it is a very important one. Choose a veterinarian you feel comfortable with. Most breeders stipulate a short period in which you may have your new pet checked out by a vet to approve her health.

The Big Day

When to bring your Ridgeback home requires careful planning. If you work, arrange to have a few days of vacation, and combine them with a full weekend to acclimate your pet to the household and routine. Both the puppy and the adult Ridgeback will need time to bond with you and settle in, and will need all the reassurance and guidance you can give in those first few days.

Holidays are a very bad time to bring a new pet into the household. With all of the activity and irregular scheduling that holidays usually bring, your Ridgeback will not be able to acquire any sense of belonging. Plan to be able to spend quiet, quality time with your Ridgeback to establish a solid routine, give her plenty of opportunity to rest and generally help her to feel at home.

THE IMPORTANCE OF A SCHEDULE

The single most important factor in acclimatizing your Ridgeback into your daily life is a schedule. Plan ahead how and when you will feed, exercise and play with your pet, so that she knows what to expect right from the first. Dogs thrive on routine; they feel secure knowing exactly what will happen next, and most dogs become upset when their normal schedule goes awry.

Give your new dog a chance to get used to her surroundings— the first few days in a new home should be on the quiet side.

It is very important to ensure that your new Ridgeback receives lots of quiet, sleepy time as well. Beginning a new life is very stressful, and your pet will need time to relax and think about all that is happening. Additionally, you should bear in mind that a puppy is a baby and, just like a human baby, will need more sleep than anything else for the first few months.

SUPERVISION

Your new puppy, and even adult Rhodesian Ridgebacks, will need to be constantly supervised when not confined to a crate or "puppy-proofed" area. Curiosity can easily lead to disaster, and a Ridgeback needs to be taught which toys and activities are safe and appropriate and which are not.

Before bringing any new pet into the household, view your home with an eye toward safety. Get down on the floor at "puppy level" and look again. The view is quite different from down below! The trouble a Ridgeback will dream up will astound you, and while it is all very

57

innocently done, the results of chewing on something harmful are devastating. Being careful also protects your clothing, shoes and other belongings from sharp teeth and powerful jaws. Puppy-proof your home as if for a young child, for a curious baby is exactly what you are getting!

You will also need to consider the best and most effective method to supervise your Ridgeback while maintaining your household routine. Naturally, your pup will be in her crate when you can't supervise, but you should also consider limiting her to a small area of the house until she is grown up enough to be deemed trustworthy. Baby gates are inexpensive and work beautifully to confine your pup to the same room with the family so that someone always knows what she is doing.

Your yard can be your Ridgeback's amusement park—if you have it well-fenced.

Preparing the Yard

Shutting your Ridgeback out of doors away from the family is not a substitute for supervision and training. Your yard can also be hazardous to a curious pup or adult. Does your garage contain paint, gasoline, antifreeze or other chemicals? Are sharp tools or blades stored there? Do you have a deck made of treated lumber? Is there cocoa mulch around your plants? All of these are very dangerous to a Ridgeback when her curiosity or taste buds lead her into mischief. Use the same puppy-proofing techniques employed inside the house to ensure your dog's safety while she enjoys the outdoors.

Part of keeping your yard safe is ensuring that it is escape-proof. Ridgebacks are champion jumpers, easily able to clear a four-foot fence. A minimum of 6-foot-high fencing is required to keep your Ridgeback safely contained. Solid wood fencing is the best choice if you live in a residential area. A solid fence prevents your Ridgeback from viewing exciting things to chase, explore or bark at while confined in her own yard. It helps keep her happy and content in her own space.

Keep Your Breeder's Number Handy

In the event that something should go wrong, or if you have any questions, the first person to call is your Ridgeback's breeder. His knowledge is extensive, and many times he will have specialized information about Ridgebacks that even your vet or obedience trainer is not familiar with.

If you are unable to speak to the breeder, contact your veterinarian or obedience trainer. Since you have established relationships with these people prior to bringing your Ridgeback home, they should also be available to answer questions. Never be afraid to ask for help! Most people are pleased to offer their assistance, especially when they are acquainted with you and your Ridgeback.

HOUSEHOLD DANGERS

Curious puppies and inquisitive dogs get into trouble not because they are bad, but simply because they want to investigate the world around them. It's our job to protect our dogs from harmful substances, like the following:

In the Garage

antifreeze

garden supplies, like snail and slug bait, pesticides, fertilizers and mouse and rat poisons

In the House

cleaners, especially pine oil

perfumes, colognes and aftershaves

medications and vitamins

office and craft supplies

electric cords

chicken and turkey bones

chocolate and onions

some house and garden plants, like ivy, oleander and poinsettia

chapter 5

Feeding
Your
Rhodesian
Ridgeback

With the great variety of dog foods currently available, the advertisements and conflicting advice, it is easy to become confused. But feeding your Ridgeback correctly is not complicated if you follow a few basic guidelines and use your common sense.

Choosing a Dog Food

Dry food (kibble) and wet food (canned) are the two basic types of dog food that are widely available. There are pros and cons to both types. Regardless of the food you choose, check the labels carefully to ensure that the legend "100 percent nutritionally complete" appears. Several established regulatory agencies perform food analysis to determine whether or not a particular food meets minimum nutrition standards. The American Animal Feed Control Officials (AAFCO) is one such group. Any nutritionally complete food (canned or dry) will have been tested and approved, and a statement to the effect will appear on the package.

Dry Food

I prefer feeding dry kibble rather than canned food for several reasons. Dry food helps keep your Ridgeback's teeth clean by scraping them as the dog eats. Dry food is less expensive than canned, and a dog needs to eat less of it, since many canned foods are nearly 75 percent water. Additionally, crunching on dry food may satisfy at least some of your pet's urge to chew. Since it takes longer for your Ridgeback to eat dry food, it also allows the dog to feel as if he has eaten more by the time he is finished.

Canned Food

Ridgebacks love the taste and smell of canned food. Because it contains meat, meat by-products and broth in a very appealing form, some people feel that it is closer to a "natural" diet than dry food.

However, canned food can be used as a complete diet only if the food is very carefully chosen. Many canned foods are intended as supplements to dry food, and not as total nutrition. Unless there is a very specific reason why your Ridgeback must have canned food as a sole

HOW TO READ THE DOG FOOD LABEL

With so many choices on the market, how can you be sure you are feeding the right food to your dog? The information is all there on the label—if you know what you're looking for.

Look for the nutritional claim right up top. Is the food "100 percent nutritionally complete"? If so, it's for nearly all life stages; "growth and maintenance," on the other hand, is for early development. Puppy foods and foods for senior dogs are specially marked.

Ingredients are listed in descending order by weight. The first three or four ingredients will tell you the bulk of what the food contains. Look for the highest-quality ingredients, like meats and grains, to be among them.

The Guaranteed Analysis tells you what levels of protein, fat, fiber and moisture are in the food, in that order. These numbers won't tell you much about the quality of the food. Nutritional value is in the dry matter, not the moisture content.

In many ways, seeing is believing. If your dog has bright eyes, a shiny coat, a good appetite and a good energy level, chances are his diet's fine. Your dog's breeder and your veterinarian are good sources of advice if you're still not sure which food is appropriate.

nutrition source, feed it only as an occasional flavoring agent on a good grade of dry food.

EVALUATING FAT AND PROTEIN PERCENTAGES

The percentage of fat and protein in the food is an important part of the label.

Protein

The correct amounts of protein and fat will provide your dog with energy and keep his coat shiny.

As a general guideline, the average adult Ridgeback should be eating a food with a protein content between 20 percent and 26 percent. The corresponding fat content should be between 12 percent and 16 percent. While protein is necessary for bone and muscle growth and maintenance of healthy body tissues, high protein food is not necessary for the average pet. Very active

dogs, or dogs under stress, will require more protein. But unless your Ridgeback is competing in performance events, in the show ring or caring for a litter of puppies, extra protein is probably not appropriate.

Fat

The fat content in your Ridgeback's food is also important. Fat is just what it is—fat! Fat is necessary for healthy coat and skin, and for maintaining energy levels. But excess fat in the diet will end up back in its original form, on your Ridgeback! Avoid foods in which the fat to protein ratio is very high.

Feeding Puppies

Many breeders and vets will recommend that you feed your baby Ridgeback a high-quality puppy food. There are two schools of thought regarding puppy food. While it is true that growing puppies need extra vitamins and minerals to ensure proper nutrition, high protein is not necessarily the best idea. Ridgebacks are large dogs, and during certain stages of puppyhood grow very rapidly. By controlling the amount of protein intake, you can either speed up or slow down, to a certain extent, the growth rate of bone and muscle. It is now generally agreed that too much growth too quickly can contribute to skeletal problems like panosteitis and possibly hip and elbow dysplasia. Thus, high-protein puppy foods are the cause of some controversy.

Choosing a Nutritious Food

So now that you have made some decisions regarding what type of food to give your Ridgeback and are ready to compare ingredients and labels, you still need to choose a nutritionally complete, balanced, high-quality food.

Not all dog foods are nutritionally equal, and different breeds fare better or worse on different brands. Chances are good that the breeder has investigated several of the better brands of dog food available and will be able to give you pointers on which brands work well for Ridgebacks. Once you have chosen a good-quality food, your Ridgeback will be set for life. Dry dog food and water is all he truly needs to stay healthy and happy. Unless your veterinarian advises vitamin or mineral supplements for a special reason, these are not necessary for a well-nourished dog.

Growing puppies have special nutritional needs that you should discuss with your veterinarian.

TABLE SCRAPS

Supplementing your Ridgeback's food with table scraps or other "extras" is also unnecessary. If you choose to give a little extra as a treat, that is fine, as long as it does not become routine. Adding table scraps, canned food or other "people food" only encourages your Ridgeback not to eat his own food. He will learn that if he refuses to eat and waits long enough, you will break down and give him the "good stuff." Since you'll be spending good money on a nutritionally complete diet to ensure his good health, make sure he eats it.

Never feed your Ridgeback anything while you are sitting at the dinner table. It won't take long before you'll have a sad-eyed, drooling, whining Ridgeback resting his chin on your dinner table, and begging is a hard habit to break once a dog acquires it.

Your Ridgeback might be willing to share his dinner with Fluffy, but I wouldn't count on it.

The Importance of Water

Your Ridgeback should have fresh water available at all times. In addition to providing water, I recommend adding water into your Ridgeback's food at each meal. Measure out his portion of food, then add just enough fresh water to cover the kibble. You do not need to allow the food to soak or get soggy; give the dry food and water to your dog right away.

NO COCOA FOR FIDO

Never give your Ridgeback chocolate in any form as a treat. Chocolate contains a substance called theobromine, which dogs are unable to digest properly, and even a small amount of chocolate can cause severe illness and even death for your pet.

How Often—How Much?

Please be sure to read this section thoroughly! Feeding your dog is more than simply putting food in a dish and walking away. Monitoring exactly how much your Ridgeback eats, and when, is an important part of maintaining his health.

A Mealtime Schedule

Start with a feeding schedule and stick with it. Puppies should be fed three times per day until approximately 6 months of age. At that time they can be switched to two meals per day, and remain on this schedule for the rest of their lives. Feeding your pet twice a day is easier on the digestive system than giving one large meal. Also, it allows you to keep track of exactly what your dog is eating, and how much.

I always joke that if my Ridgebacks are not eating, they are most likely dead! While this is obvious exaggeration, it is not far from the truth. The only thing in the world your Ridgeback will love more than he loves you is his dinner! So if your Ridgeback is not eating, it is a sure sign that something is amiss.

Make your pet's food available for no more than twenty minutes at a time. A normal Ridgeback will not leave it in his dish for any more than sixty seconds! However, if he occasionally does skip a meal, take it away and give him nothing else to eat (no biscuits or goodies!) until the next regular mealtime. This will teach your pet to eat what he is given and when it is given to him, and will discourage finicky eating habits.

Your Rhodesian should have a healthy appetite and welcome mealtime.

How Much to Feed

For a large dog, you may be surprised at how little food an adult Ridgeback actually needs to keep in top physical shape. Generally, my adult females will eat between 3 to 4 level measuring cups of food per day. My males eat approximately 4 to 6 cups per day. Much of this depends on an individual dog's activity level, age and body metabolism. Puppies may eat slightly more during growth phases, but generally fall within the same range.

Although the Ridgeback is described as a substantial animal, this does not correspond with fat! In proper weight and body condition, you should just be able to see the shadow of each of your pet's ribs. If you place your hands on either side of his rib cage, you should be able to feel the individual ribs but not the hollows between them.

TO SUPPLEMENT OR NOT TO SUPPLEMENT?

If you're feeding your dog a diet that's correct for his developmental stage and he's alert, healthy looking and neither over- nor underweight, you don't need to add supplements. These include table scraps as well as vitamins and minerals. In fact, unless you are a nutrition expert, using food supplements can actually hurt a growing puppy. For example, mixing too much calcium into your dog's food can lead to musculo-skeletal disorders. Educating yourself about the quantity of vitamins and minerals your dog needs to be healthy will help you determine what needs to be supplemented. If you have any concerns about the nutritional quality of the food you're feeding, discuss them with your veterinarian.

MANAGING THE OVERWEIGHT DOG

If you discover that you have overfed your pet, a gradual reduction in the amount of food you give, plus an increase in exercise, will usually take care of the unwanted pounds.

Most people who overfeed their dog do so by giving him too many extra goodies or the wrong kind of treats. If you give your pet quite a few treats during the course of the day, you may want to give those treats in the form of raw vegetables, instead of "doggy junk food." Carrots, broccoli, cauliflower, fresh green beans, even pieces of apple or pear are big favorites in my house. Not only are they low in fat and healthy for your pet, they are appreciated just as much as commercial dog treats.

When buying dog treats, be sure to read the ingredients on the label. Just as you would do for yourself, avoid treats that are composed mainly of sugars and cereals. A treat does not have to be a large portion of anything. Your Ridgeback will be happy to receive even a little nibble. It is more the idea that you are giving him something special than the need for extra food that appeals to him.

Grooming
Your
Rhodesian
Ridgeback

One of the best things about Rhodesian Ridgebacks is that they are wash-and-wear dogs in every sense of the word. Grooming a Ridgeback is simple, fast and fun for both owner and dog. Because it is so pleasurable, grooming is a special bonding time, and should be a part of your daily routine with your pet.

The basic grooming tools for a Rhodesian Ridgeback are few and simple. These include a rubber curry brush or hound glove, a dog nail clipper for large dogs, a small pair of blunt-tipped scissors and a soft washcloth or hand towel. You will also need a good all-purpose dog shampoo for the occasional bath, and a toothbrush and toothpaste made especially for dogs' dental needs.

A Ridgeback puppy may be too wiggly and excited for you to attempt grooming sessions of more than a few minutes at a time, but with patience and understanding she will grow to love the special attention and eventually will stand or sit quietly for you.

GROOMING TOOLS

pin brush
slicker brush
flea comb
towel
mat rake
grooming glove
scissors
nail clippers
tooth-cleaning equipment
shampoo
conditioner
clippers

Coat Care

The Ridgeback's coat is naturally tidy and odor-free. Unlike with many other breeds, you won't need to spend a great deal of time looking after your dog's coat.

BATHING

Although you won't have to bathe your Ridgeback frequently, she will need the occasional scrub. This is easily accomplished in your bathtub. Fill the tub with 4 to 6 inches of warm water.

Chances are good that your Ridgeback will learn to enjoy bath time.

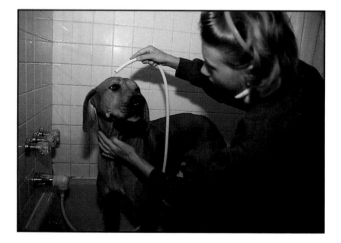

Use a large plastic cup or a spray attachment to wet your Ridgeback well all over. An old washcloth comes in handy to get areas like her belly, legs, throat and chest wet. Always move slowly and carefully so as not to startle your dog or cause her to slip in the tub; Ridgebacks have incredible memories, and a bad experience could make bathing her difficult for a long time to come.

After she is thoroughly soaked, rub a little shampoo into her coat and lather it well all over her body. Be sure to rinse all the shampoo out, being careful not to get any in her eyes or ears. Normally I do not use shampoo on a Ridgeback's face, but just wash it gently with a cloth and some warm water.

Have several large towels ready, as you will certainly need more than one! Rub your dog all over with the towels making sure she is quite dry.

BRUSHING

A good brushing every day will keep your pet's coat and skin in top condition. Start with the rubber curry or hound glove. Using firm but gentle strokes, brush your Ridgeback all over in a circular motion. You may brush your

Most Ridgebacks like the feeling of being brushed and you'll both be pleased at how tidy your dog appears afterward.

dog's ridge and coat in the "wrong" direction—it will not hurt her. Be sure to cover your dog's entire body with the brush, including legs, underside and tail. Gently brush her head, too. Most Ridgebacks love the feel of the brush and your dog may actually lean her body into it.

Be sure to check carefully as you brush for any skin irritation, scratches or sores, and also for any signs of fleas, ticks or other external parasites.

CLIPPING TOENAILS

Make sure you start trimming your pet's nails right from the time she is very small and you will have less trouble. If your pet struggles the first few times you cut her nails, or if you are unsure of where and how to cut, ask your veterinarian, a groomer or your dog's breeder to show you how until you feel comfortable.

Dental Care

The final step in your daily grooming routine should be dental care. To keep your Ridgeback's teeth clean, you may use a regular toothbrush, or purchase one of the several different styles made especially for dogs.

You can also help your Ridgeback clean her teeth by giving her chew toys that are especially designed to aid in dental care. Hard, crunchy biscuits and dry kibble dog food will help keep tartar from accumulating as well.

chapter 7

Keeping Your Rhodesian Ridgeback Healthy

Your veterinarian is your partner in maintaining the good health of your Ridgeback. She can advise you on first aid, preventive care and specific problems that you may encounter, as well as providing your pet's annual checkups and vaccinations. A veterinarian can also be a valuable resource for other important information, like advice on where to find a good obedience trainer or dog club.

Choosing a Veterinarian

If you have other pets, you should already have a vet that you know and trust. If this is to be your first pet, you will need to begin your search for a veterinarian several weeks before your Ridgeback is scheduled to join you. If you are acquiring a Ridgeback from a source in your area, ask which veterinarian the seller uses, and consider following that recommendation.

If your breeder's veterinarian is not an option, try to find a local vet who is familiar with Ridgebacks; other local Ridgeback owners will probably have good suggestions. If all else fails, ask friends with other pets whom they have chosen, and why. Do not be afraid to call a veterinarian's office to ask questions about the practice, fee schedule, staffing during off-hours and whether the practice has treated any Ridgebacks.

Preventive health care begins very early in a puppy's life. The breeder will have provided your puppy's initial vaccinations and deworming, and should furnish you with a record of these. Make sure your vet receives a copy of this important record, so that the correct care can be given in follow-up.

Vaccines

Vaccinations can be confusing, but just like human infants, puppies are susceptible to a number of very serious and potentially fatal diseases. Puppies receive some initial immunity at birth from their mother, but by the time they are old enough to leave their dam, they should have begun receiving more complete protection in the form of vaccines. Your puppy's immunizations are vital protection, so be certain to adhere to the schedule carefully. Today, most veterinarians will usually help in this by notifying clients by mail when immunization is due.

KENNEL COUGH

Kennel cough is a contagious, debilitating condition that affects a dog's respiratory tract. Constant coughing, wheezing and sneezing is especially hard on puppies and elderly dogs. Although a number of different viral and bacterial strains can cause kennel cough, the vast majority of infections result from three particular agents: parainfluenza (see above), adenovirus-2 and Bordetella bronchiseptica. A vaccine effective against these most common causes of kennel cough is available. Although infection is still possible after vaccination, the protection afforded by the immunization is very valuable, especially if your Ridgeback is in contact with groups of strange dogs, such as in a boarding kennel, at a dog show or in an obedience class.

> ### YOUR PUPPY'S VACCINES
>
> Vaccines are given to prevent your dog from getting an infectious disease like canine distemper or rabies. Vaccines are the ultimate preventive medicine: They're given before your dog ever gets the disease so as to protect him from the disease. That's why it is necessary for your dog to be vaccinated routinely. Puppy vaccines start at 8 weeks of age for the five-in-one DHLPP vaccine and are given every three to four weeks until the puppy is 16 weeks old. Your veterinarian will put your puppy on a proper schedule and will re-mind you when to bring in your dog for shots.

RABIES

Rabies is probably the best known and most feared disease because it occurs in all warm-blooded animals and is transmissible to man. In animals, the death rate is 100 percent once the symptoms of the disease appear. Changes in personality and behavior of both wild and domestic animals are the recognizable symptoms of rabies, but by the time these are noticeable it is already too late. Rabies is spread through contact with infected body fluids, most often through scratch or bite wounds. Puppies should receive an initial rabies vaccination by no later than 6 months of age, although laws vary from state to state regarding when dogs must receive their first immunization. Your vet will be able to advise you what your state's requirements are. Dogs must receive a second immunization one year following the initial vaccine, and then should receive boosters every two to three years thereafter.

Internal Parasites

Along with yearly vaccinations, your Ridgeback will require regular testing and possibly treatment for worms or organisms causing coccidiosis or giardiasis. The following is a brief overview of the most common parasites seen in dogs.

Roundworms occur with a good deal of frequency in both puppies and adult dogs. Most puppies will need to be treated for roundworms since they are passed from dam to pups before birth and later through her milk. Heavy infestations of roundworms can be fatal.

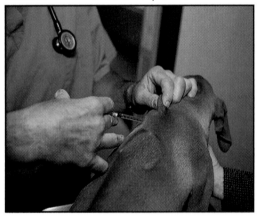

Infected puppies will have dull coats, diarrhea and appear thin yet pot-bellied. Round-worms are visible in your pet's stool and look like white spag-hetti strands. How-ever, a fecal exam will detect the presence of roundworms long before you see them in the stool, so do not neglect this important test at your Ridgeback's regular visits to the veterinarian.

Hookworms cause iron deficiency anemia in dogs since this worm attaches itself to the intestines and feeds on the blood of its host. Hookworms are also transmissible to people and can be acquired either through infected feces or from contaminated soil in affected areas. Pups can be infected before birth from their dam. Hook-worms are not visible to the naked eye; a fecal exam is required to diagnose this debilitating parasite.

Whipworms are one of the most difficult parasites to treat since eggs are not always visible on a fecal exam and diagnosis is problematic. Weight loss and diarrhea are the most common signs of whipworm infestation, although admittedly these symptoms can represent a number of potential problems. Whipworms are not visible in the stool, and often treatment is necessary on a presumed diagnosis since they are so difficult to detect.

This parasite is quite debilitating if left untreated, but there are several medications that are effective against whipworms and the other types of worms described above.

Once a dog becomes infected, it can be difficult to eradicate the problem, and repeated treatment is usually necessary.

Tapeworms are one of the easiest problems to diagnose, as the worms are visible as white, rice-like particles seen in stools or around the anus. Tapeworms are usually transmitted to your pet from fleas, so good control of fleas is also important in controlling a tapeworm infestation. Flea control alone is not enough to clear up the problem, however, so if you suspect your Ridgeback has acquired tapeworm, a visit to your vet for proper treatment is indicated.

Heartworm infestation varies from the other common parasites in that the heartworm inhabits your pet's heart muscle, rather than the intestinal tract, and requires vigilant preventive measures. Mosquitoes infected with heartworm pass the larvae on to your pet when they bite. The larvae migrate to the right ventricle of the heart and grow to be adult worms.

Common internal parasites (l-r): roundworm, whipworm, tapeworm and hookworm.

Diagnosis is by a blood test that shows the presence of microfilariae. Unfortunately, by the time the microfilariae are detectable in the blood, the infection is already 6 or 7 months old, and your Ridgeback has adult worms in his heart. These worms clog 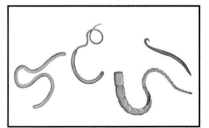 the heart and restrict blood flow, resulting in a number of health problems and eventually a fatal heart attack.

Treatment for a dog infected with heartworm is difficult. The most commonly used treatment is arsenic, which kills the adult worms. However, arsenic is also poisonous to your pet, and the treatment is risky. Other methods are being developed, but the very best cure is prevention. Your veterinarian can offer you once-a-month medication that will keep your Ridgeback from contracting heartworm.

External Parasites

FLEAS

Fleas are tiny, biting insects that feed on blood. A heavy infestation of fleas can debilitate any dog by causing anemia, and can contribute to the death of an older dog or puppy. When a flea bites, its saliva irritates the skin, causing your pet to scratch, which is often the first sign of a problem. Fleabites can cause an allergic reaction in some dogs, with redness, inflammation, hair loss and open, weeping sores (called "hot spots") caused by constant scratching, biting and licking at the irritated skin.

The flea is a die-hard pest.

Many people are under the impression that living with a dog means living with fleas; however, a flea infestation is never acceptable. Fleas are intermediary carriers of disease and other parasites, including tapeworm, and fleas will readily bite humans as well as animals.

Daily grooming sessions are a good time to check your Ridgeback for any signs of fleas. Flea dirt is usually found near the tail and along the spine, while fleas themselves can be seen on the skin, especially in the groin, belly and anal regions.

There are a number of effective flea-killing products on the market. Flea shampoo will kill the fleas on the dog but will not prevent more fleas from jumping on. Flea dips, sprays and powders have more long-lasting and preventive effects but must be used with care. Most flea-killing products contain chemicals that can also be harmful to your Ridgeback; to poison the flea, you must also poison the dog. All flea products should be used strictly according to the manufacturer's directions. If there is any doubt, call your veterinarian for advice.

After ensuring your Ridgeback is flea-free and comfortable, you must treat the environment to kill the adult, egg-laying fleas. The best products are less toxic to your pet, your family and the environment, and contain IGR (insect growth regulator). IGR chemicals work on the reproductive system of the flea and prevent the adolescents from becoming mature enough to reproduce.

If you do not already have one in place, you will need to implement a preventive program. There are several very good products available that will ensure your Ridgeback stays free of fleas and ticks. Monthly pills or liquid applied to your pet's skin are proven safe and will effectively prevent infestation and kill fleas and ticks. If started before flea season, you will never need to deal with the trouble of eradicating the pests. Your veterinarian can help you choose the product that will work best for your dog.

TICKS

Ticks pose a very serious health threat to both dogs and humans because they carry and transmit several catastrophic diseases. Like fleas, ticks feed on blood, but unlike fleas, they slowly gorge on blood over a period of several days. Ticks embed their entire head underneath the Ridgeback's skin and commence feeding. After feeding, the female tick drops off the host to lay her eggs, up to 12,000 at a time! The most common areas to find ticks on your pet are the head and neck, around the base of the ears (be sure to check  inside the ears as well), in the armpits and between the toes. Although they prefer warm, protected areas of the dog, a tick will attach itself anywhere it can climb on, so watch carefully for these predators, and remove them promptly.

Use tweezers to remove ticks from your dog.

Ticks are easier to remove from your Ridgeback (or yourself) if they are killed first. A flea and tick spray is fastest, although you must remember to exercise caution when using any toxic chemical. Isopropyl alcohol will also kill ticks, although it will take a bit longer. Apply any killing agent with a cotton ball or other applicator; do not touch the chemical or the tick itself. Once the tick is dead, it can easily be removed by grasping the body with a pair of tweezers and pulling straight away from the skin.

The monthly flea preventives discussed above will also help to prevent ticks, and nearly all flea control products are effective against ticks as well. Additionally, special collars are now available that help prevent tick infestation, although care should be taken to ensure that your dog does not chew on these collars, as they are toxic when ingested.

EAR MITES

Ear mites cause itchiness and ear infection, and are highly contagious. Scratching the ears, shaking the head and loss of balance (due to infection) are signs of ear mite infestation. Although distressing, ear mites can be treated safely with medication to kill the mites, along with antibiotics for the infection.

Health Concerns of Ridgebacks

One of the best characteristics of Ridgebacks is that they are relatively free from the health problems that afflict so many other breeds. However, there are a few genetic and congenital conditions to be aware of, as well as some specific ailments that can threaten your pet's life. As with any question about your Ridgeback, contact your breeder and/or veterinarian for further information about health conditions.

DERMOID SINUS

Congenital conditions are present at birth. For the Rhodesian Ridgeback, the most important of these is the dermoid sinus. The dermoid sinus is a hollow tube of skin which begins at a pore (opening) on the skin and continues down through the skin and muscle layers directly to the spinal cord. This tube of skin may or may not contain hair follicles and hair growth along its length, and grows, sheds particles and replenishes itself exactly as the skin on the outside of the dog does. This normal rejuvenation process eventually causes the tube to become obstructed with dead hair and skin cells, which the body tries to expel. Fluid collection and infection is the result, and can lead to nondraining abscesses, bacterial infection of the spinal cord and eventually a painful death.

Thankfully, the dermoid sinus is detectable immediately after birth either by palpating or shaving the puppy. An experienced Ridgeback breeder will know how to detect the condition, while unfortunately many veterinarians are unaware of the problem or how to detect it. Puppies diagnosed with the dermoid sinus are normally euthanized.

Occasionally a dermoid sinus will be overlooked. Surgical removal is possible, but the operation can be delicate. Moreover, the dermoid sinus can grow back, even after what appears to be a successful removal. Any Ridgeback who survives a dermoid sinus should be spayed or neutered since there is strong evidence for a genetic component to the incidence of the condition.

HYPOTHYROIDISM

Hypothyroidism is another congenital disorder that primarily affects medium-size to large breeds. Rarely seen in Ridgebacks in years past, it has recently become more of a concern. A deficiency of the thyroid gland causes lowered metabolic rates, which affects all organ systems. Symptoms include dullness, lethargy, heat seeking due to low body temperatures, dry skin and hair loss. Most dogs do not show symptoms of hypothyroidism until they are mature, usually between 4 and 10 years of age. This disease can be difficult to diagnose, as many illnesses show similar symptoms; however, blood testing of thyroid hormone levels is available. Hypothyroidism can be controlled with medication prescribed by your veterinarian.

HIP DYSPLASIA

Hip dysplasia is a crippling deformity of the hip joint that is at least partly hereditary and partly exacerbated by environmental factors. Rhodesian Ridgebacks are not as susceptible to hip dysplasia as other breeds of similar size; however, it is still of tremendous concern. Good breeding practices can help to keep hip dysplasia under control. When buying your Ridgeback, be certain to obtain copies of the OFA (Orthopedic Foundation for Animals) certificates on both his parents. While this does not guarantee that your Ridgeback will be dysplasia-free, it is important to know that the parents are free of this disease and less likely to have passed it to their offspring.

Hip joint pain and decreased activity are signs of a possible problem. Reduction of or hesitation in activities such as sitting, jumping, climbing stairs or a show of reluctance or pain on arising from a lying position are signs of possible dysplasia. Your vet can x-ray your Ridgeback's hips and submit the films to the Orthopedic Foundation for Animals for evaluation of hip dysplasia. An affected dog will develop secondary osteoarthritis, which is painful and debilitating. There is little to be done for this condition other than pain control. In very severe cases, the femoral head (the top of the dog's hind leg bone that connects to the hip) can be surgically replaced, but the surgery is expensive, not always successful and very painful.

BLOAT

Bloat is the common name for gastric torsion, the dreaded killer of large and deep-chested dogs. Unfortunately, Rhodesian Ridgebacks are among the susceptible breeds. In an episode of bloat, the stomach fills with gas and fluid and can actually twist on its own axis and entirely block itself. This twisting is known as torsion or volvulus and will kill a dog in an extremely short time. Signs that your Ridgeback is bloating include panting, restlessness, indications of extreme pain, attempts at vomiting and rapid visible distension of the stomach, which becomes hard and tympanic.

If your Ridgeback bloats, immediate emergency veterinary care is the only hope of saving his life. If the stomach has not twisted, the gas and fluid may be pumped out of the dog's stomach through a tube. Once torsion occurs, emergency surgery to repair the stomach is the only option.

There are no good answers as to why or how bloat occurs, but some preventive measures have been identified. Feed your Ridgeback two smaller meals each day, as opposed to one large meal (see Chapter 5). Mix food with water to slow down eating and distension of food in your pet's stomach. Do not allow strenuous activity for a period of time immediately before and after meals. And follow an immunization schedule which does not overload an immature puppy's system with too many vaccines at one time (see the section on vaccines at the beginning of this chapter).

Fortunately, Ridgebacks suffer from relatively few genetic maladies.

COMMON INJURIES

Other problems specific to Ridgebacks include ear and tail injuries. Although not life-threatening, an open wound to an ear or tail requires immediate attention because this can be difficult to heal.

Ear Injuries

If your Ridgeback sustains an injury to his ear that causes bleeding, first thoroughly clean and disinfect the wound. If it does not require a trip to the vet for stitches, pack the wound with styptic powder, which helps the blood to clot, then cover with sterile gauze.

The ear should then be secured in place, either by taping it on top of the head or by taping it to the opposite ear underneath the chin.

Tail Injuries

Open wounds to the tail are likewise very difficult to heal since wagging the tail vigorously or banging it against furniture and doorways reopens the wound. For small wounds, you may pack the cleaned and disinfected wound with styptic powder. Then cover with a regular adhesive bandage like you would use on your own skin. A day or two of confinement to a crate will also protect the wound from reinjury and help speed the healing process.

Spay or Neuter Your Ridgeback

Some of the most devastating health problems your Ridgeback may face are also the easiest to prevent. Spaying or neutering your pet at an early age will prevent several common forms of cancer, as well as catastrophic infections of the reproductive system.

You may want to crate an injured dog to keep him still and promote healing.

Unspayed females are 200 times more likely to develop mammary tumors than females that were spayed before coming into heat for the first time. Thus, early spaying is by far the most effective preventive available! By waiting until after your bitch goes through one heat cycle before spaying, you have already substantially increased the risk of mammary tumors. And the longer your bitch remains intact, the greater the chances that mammary tumors will become malignant. Spaying also prevents most ovary, uterine and external genital tumors.

Sterilization (spaying) of your female Ridgeback involves surgical removal of the ovaries, fallopian tubes and uterus. The surgery is done under general anesthesia, and usually requires an overnight stay under veterinary supervision. Recovery time is short, only seven to ten days, and your pet will be her happy, bouncy self again, none the worse for the experience. Your veterinarian will help you to decide the most appropriate age for this procedure to be performed, although spaying before 6 months of age will ensure that no heat cycles occur.

The female in heat is an experience most people would happily forego! Most bitches experience two heat cycles per year, accompanied by copious menstrual bleeding for a full three weeks, which is messy and inconvenient to say the least. She will need to be kept under lock and key every minute since the males will come literally from miles around once they catch her scent, and will camp out on your lawn until your female's heat cycle is over.

In males, neutering prevents testicular and prostate cancer, prostate infection, perianal tumors and hernias arising from prostate problems. Prostate infections are hormonally triggered and difficult to treat. Once a dog has incurred a prostatic infection, he will usually have recurrent problems from that point on. Neutering will eliminate that possibility.

Neutering your male Ridgeback also eliminates the behavioral problems associated with the sex drive. Escaping the safety of his yard to search for females in heat will be eliminated, as will the howling, whining, pacing and refusal to eat of a sexually frustrated entire male. Territorial marking behaviors (leg-lifting indoors and at other inappropriate locations) will be greatly reduced, as will aggression toward other males. A neutered male is a happier, calmer, more enjoyable pet.

Neutering involves surgical removal of the testicles, which produce sperm and control steroid hormone secretion. Neutering is a simple procedure, with rapid healing time. Most dogs are back to normal within three days following the procedure!

The old wives' tales suggest that spaying or neutering will make dogs fat and lazy is simply untrue. Actually, only overeating and a lack of exercise will make a dog fat and lazy! A spayed or neutered Ridgeback is a more devoted and enjoyable pet, and a healthier animal.

If Your Ridgeback Is Sick

Any signs of illness in your Ridgeback require your immediate evaluation and action. If you think that your Ridgeback is not feeling his best, try to pinpoint exactly why you think this by observing the following:

- Is your Ridgeback eating normally? If a Ridgeback is not eating, it is usually a sign of an important problem!

- Is your Ridgeback passing normal stools? Check for diarrhea, loose stools, blood or mucus in or on the stool, and whether the stool appears too small or hard. Also look carefully for foreign objects or parasites contained in the stool.

Your Ridgeback's stoicism is not necessarily an asset—you must be vigilant in observing your dog for signs of illness or injury.

- Does your Ridgeback have a fever? Instructions on taking your pet's temperature appear later in this chapter.

- Does your Ridgeback have swelling or lumps, or areas that are abnormally warm to the touch anywhere on his body?

- Is your Ridgeback limping, or favoring or protecting any particular part of his body?

- What is your Ridgeback doing, or not doing, that is out of the ordinary and makes you feel there is a problem?

By making careful note of the above conditions, you will be better prepared to help your veterinarian care for your pet in the event this becomes necessary. Just as with your family, some conditions or illnesses are slight and can be managed at home. Others require immediate veterinary attention. Since your Ridgeback can not tell you how serious the problem is, *always* contact your vet if you have any questions. Remember that as a breed, Rhodesian Ridgebacks are very stoic; often they will not react to pain or illness until an emergency situation develops. Any suspicion on your part that your pet may be ill or hurt requires your careful attention to determine the nature of the problem.

Once, while observing a litter of puppies playing in the yard, one little female came over and sat quietly at my feet, leaning in close to be cuddled. Immediately my suspicions were aroused. This pup was one of the most boisterous in the litter and almost never sat quietly anywhere! A careful check revealed a rapidly swelling bee sting that required immediate first aid. Learn to interpret what your Ridgeback is trying to tell you. Sometimes your powers of observation can make a critical difference.

Emergency!

With dogs you should always be prepared for emergencies before they happen. Part of establishing a relationship with your Ridgeback's veterinarian includes knowing what to expect in an emergency. Is there a vet on call during nonbusiness hours, or is there a local emergency clinic that you will be referred to? Know who to call and keep the number posted by your phone so it will be available when you need it.

YOUR DOG'S FIRST AID KIT

A first aid kit for your Ridgeback should include:

Activated charcoal tablets
Adhesive tape (2 rolls, 2 inches wide)
Antibiotic ointment (ophthalmic for eyes, and triple antibiotic for skin)
Antidiarrhea medication
Antihistamine for insect bites
Aspirin (buffered or enteric coated, *not* ibuprofen or aspirin substitutes)
Bandages (rolls of 2-inch-wide gauze, large sterile gauze pads, and outer wrapping material)
Cotton balls
Flea and tick spray
Hydrogen peroxide (3 percent)
Latex gloves
Marked syringe (for dosing medication)
Muzzle
Petroleum jelly
Rectal thermometer
Rubbing alcohol
Scissors
Soft towels
Styptic powder
Tourniquet
Tweezers

Prepare a first-aid kit especially for your pet. Many of the items you will need are both inexpensive and commonly found in most homes. Be sure to buy duplicate items as required, and keep them separate from the medical supplies you keep for your human family so they are always available when you need them. See the sidebar for a list of items you should keep on hand.

Emergency situations usually require prompt action on your part, even before transporting your Ridgeback to the vet for help. Just as with humans, the most important thing in an emergency is to stay calm and act quickly. Stabilize your Ridgeback and the situation, and immediately call your vet. The following information will be important in an emergency but should *never* be considered a substitute for your veterinarian's care and advice.

HOW TO APPLY A MUZZLE

Use a scarf or old hose to make a temporary muzzle, as shown.

No matter how much your Ridgeback loves and trusts you, if he is injured or afraid, he may bite! Traumatic injuries and painful illnesses (such as bloat) require that your pet be muzzled so that you and your vet can treat him safely and stop the pain.

Any long, soft piece of cloth can be utilized. A pair of pantyhose, a strong gauze bandage or even your Ridgeback's leash can serve as a temporary muzzle in an emergency. Put the middle portion of the muzzle material underneath your dog's chin, and tie over the top of his muzzle, making sure his mouth is shut. Cross the material and wrap around your dog's muzzle again, this time tying it under his chin. Then take each end of the cloth and pull it back underneath and behind the ears, tying it again at the back of his head. Make sure the muzzle is tight enough that it will not slip off, but not so tight that it will restrict breathing, especially if there is any indication of choking or shortness of breath.

TAKING YOUR DOG'S TEMPERATURE

A dog's correct body temperature is between 101° and 102°F. Fever in a dog is an indication of something serious, and a simple rectal thermometer from your local drug store is all that is required.

Shake down the thermometer and coat the end with petroleum jelly. Lift your Ridgeback's tail and insert the tip of the thermometer into the rectum about one inch. Hold onto the thermometer! If your Ridgeback squirms, it may fall out and break and cause injury. Have someone hold his head if he will not stand or lie quietly for this procedure. After approximately three minutes, remove the thermometer, wipe it off with a cloth and read the temperature. Be sure to disinfect the thermometer with rubbing alcohol on a cotton ball after each use.

MANAGING TRAUMA

Injuries resulting from being hit by a car, fractures, dogfights or bite wounds from wild animals all require immediate attention. These situations should always be handled with extreme care, as your Ridgeback will probably be in considerable pain. Applying a muzzle is the first step, so you can safely stabilize your pet and transport him to the vet for emergency care.

If your Ridgeback is struck by a car, fractures, large open wounds and internal organ damage and bleeding are all possible results. Time is of the essence to save your pet's life.

If you suspect broken bones in any part of your Ridgeback's body, try to stabilize the area as well as possible. For a broken leg, apply a splint using a length of wood, heavy cardboard or other stiff material. Align the leg to the splint, then wrap in a soft covering to help prevent further trauma or infection. Tape or tie firmly in place until you reach the veterinarian's office.

Whenever possible, place your Ridgeback on a stretcher before moving him to help prevent further injuries. Again, a large board or piece of heavy cardboard can be used as a stretcher. If nothing else is available, use a sheet or large towel. It also helps if there are two people to carry the stretcher. Try to avoid gathering your Ridgeback up in your arms, as this can cause further injury, although if there is no other option, by all means do so!

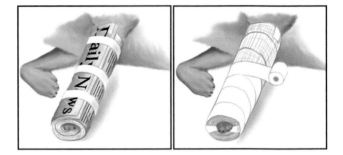

Make a temporary splint by wrapping the leg in firm casing, then bandaging it.

Managing Bleeding

Dogfights or encounters with wild animals can result in serious bite and scratch wounds and heavy bleeding. Bleeding needs to be addressed immediately. Apply direct pressure over the wound using a clean towel or gauze pad. Don't be afraid to press firmly! If the wound is not extremely large and not in close proximity to the head, you may pour hydrogen peroxide over it to help prevent infection. Once the bleeding is under control, immediately seek veterinary attention for further antibiotic therapy and suturing if necessary.

If heavy bleeding occurs in legs or tail, a tourniquet may be utilized to help control blood loss. Ask your veterinarian to show you how to properly apply a tourniquet so you will be prepared for this situation. If a tourniquet is used, it must be loosened approximately every fifteen minutes.

If injury is the result of an encounter with a wild animal, try to avoid contact with all bodily fluids (blood, saliva, urine, feces) as many diseases, including rabies, are transmitted in this way. Notify your veterinarian if there is any question of exposure to either your Ridgeback or yourself.

CHOKING

Choking is always life-threatening and requires immediate action. A dog can die within minutes without oxygen, so clearing the airway is of utmost importance. Normally choking occurs when a bone, toy or other object becomes lodged in your Ridgeback's throat, blocking off his air supply. If your Ridgeback is gasping for air, drooling, gagging or attempting to retch, he may be choking.

Many objects can be removed by opening your dog's mouth and putting your fingers down his throat to pull them out. You can also use large tweezers or a pair of pliers if the object is too slippery to grasp with your fingers. If you are unsuccessful, lay your Ridgeback on his side with his head and neck stretched out straight. Place the flat side of your palms just behind the rib cage, down low towards the stomach, and give several sharp thrusts, as you would do when performing the Heimlich maneuver on a person. The goal is to force the air out of the lungs and expel the object. If you must hurry to the vet, get someone to go with you and try to keep your Ridgeback's airway open by keeping the head and neck straight, pulling the tongue aside and continuing to try and expel the object.

> ### WHEN TO CALL THE VETERINARIAN
>
> In any emergency situation, you should call your veterinarian immediately. Try to stay calm when you call, and give the vet or the assistant as much information as possible before you leave for the clinic. That way, the staff will be able to take immediate, specific action when you arrive. Emergencies include:
>
> - Bleeding or deep wounds
> - Hyperthermia (overheating)
> - Shock
> - Dehydration
> - Abdominal pain
> - Burns
> - Fits
> - Unconsciousness
> - Broken bones
> - Paralysis
>
> Call your veterinarian if you suspect any health troubles.

INSECT STINGS

Insect stings can be very dangerous if your Ridgeback is allergic to them. If your pet receives a bee or wasp sting that immediately begins to swell, remove the stinger with a pair of tweezers, administer antihistamine from your first aid kit and call your veterinarian. Be especially cautious about stingers that are embedded near the nose or throat, as severe swelling can close off the airway and choke your pet.

HEATSTROKE

On a summer's day, let your dog enjoy an air-conditioned room. Don't ever leave him in a sealed-up car.

Heatstroke is another life-threatening condition that can kill your Ridgeback within minutes. Access to plenty of cool water and shade during the hot months is absolutely necessary to prevent this problem. Happily, most dogs are smart enough to pass the "dog days of summer" relaxing in the shade during hot weather, and not overexert themselves. Alternatively, your pet can be left inside your home with fans or air conditioner running.

As with all devastating conditions, puppies and elderly dogs are affected first by weather extremes, although many, many dogs die from heatstroke every year because careless owners leave them in parked cars in the sun. The temperature inside a parked car, even with the windows left open, can reach over 100°F within minutes. High temperatures quickly cause brain damage and death. *Never* leave your Ridgeback in a car during the summer months. If you can't take your dog to wherever it is you are going during a summer errand, leave him at home instead.

Treatment for heatstroke consists of immediately placing the dog in a tub of cool water, or running cool water over him using a garden hose. Try to get your pet to drink water, and monitor his temperature to make sure it is coming down. Wrap him in cold towels and rush him to the vet for emergency treatment.

POISONING

Substances that are poisonous to your Ridgeback are commonly found throughout your house and yard. You should be aware of what they are, and what to do if your dog comes in contact with them. It is common sense that chemicals like pesticides, rodent poisons, antifreeze, paint and cleaning solutions are toxic. Don't assume that a Ridgeback knows enough not to taste them—a bored adult or curious pup will amuse himself with whatever he can find, including danger-ous chemicals. Antifreeze especially is attractive to ani-mals because of its sweet taste. Keep all chemicals out of reach of your Ridgeback, just as you would do with young children.

Other lethal poisons include many common house-hold medications. For example, ibuprofen and aspirin substitutes are deadly to dogs. Never purposely give your Ridgeback any human medica-tion unless you have checked with your veterinarian to be certain it is safe.

RESPONDING TO POISONING

Symptoms of poisoning are varied but include drooling, retching, vomiting, diarrhea, glassy eyes, fixed or dilated pupils, convulsions, weakness and col-

Some of the many house-hold substances harmful to your dog.

lapse. Time is critical if your dog ingests poison. *Call your veterinarian immediately,* as many poisons can cause serious damage to your Ridgeback within minutes of ingestion. If your vet is not immediately available, you can call the 24-hour hot line of the ASPCA National Animal Poison Control Center at (800) 548-2423. The hot line is staffed by veterinarians and veterinarian tox-icology specialists. There is a fee for their service, which can be charged to your credit card. Try to deter-mine what your Ridgeback has eaten, and how much, to help your veterinarian effectively decide on the proper treatment. *Do not make your dog vomit unless instructed to do so!*

Stomach Upset

DIARRHEA

Diarrhea can be caused by many different factors, some of them minor and some of them very serious. Anytime your Ridgeback has diarrhea that contains blood, mucus, worms or foreign objects, you will need to seek a veterinarian's attention right away. Blood in the stool can be bright red, dark brown or even black in color, depending upon from which part of the digestive system it originated. So watch your Ridgeback's stool carefully for these color changes. Severe cases of diarrhea where the stool is the consistency of colored water, is constant or projectile in nature or which has a distinct odor of blood will also necessitate an immediate trip to the vet.

Minor episodes of loose stools or occasional diarrhea can usually be monitored and managed at home, unless they do not clear up within a few days. Your veterinarian can advise you which antidiarrheal medications are safe for dogs, and how much to give. Whenever your Ridgeback has diarrhea, take him off all food and water for twenty-four hours to rest the digestive tract. Then start him on a diet of boiled rice and meat (hamburger or chicken) with any fat skimmed off. Once he is feeling better, you can gradually reintroduce regular dog food, a little at a time.

With any case of diarrhea, watch carefully to see that your pet does not become dehydrated, which can occur very quickly in puppies and elderly dogs. Dehydration is always a problem and is best left for your veterinarian to treat.

VOMITING

Vomiting can be an indication of many different problems, from a simple upset stomach to ingestion of poison to a dangerous intestinal blockage. If your Ridgeback vomits, look carefully at the regurgitated material. If it contains blood, suspicious plant material or other foreign objects, or is an unusual color, call your veterinarian. It is normal for dogs to eat grass and then regurgitate; however, any matter other than grass or food is cause for alarm, as is continued or forceful, projectile vomiting.

Giving Medication

Getting your Ridgeback to take his medication does not have to be difficult. With the right bit of bribery, he will rarely give you any trouble. Since Ridgebacks are such notoriously undiscriminating eaters, the easiest method is simply to mix any medication (pills or liquids) into their regular meal. A Ridgeback may hold out for a moment or two at the smell of medicine in his food, but most will decide to gobble the meal anyway. You only need to watch and be sure he does not spit out any pills. If your pet will not take a pill in his regular meal, hide the medication inside a special treat and it will surely disappear. My all-time favorite treat for giving medication is peanut butter since it sticks to the medicine and there is little chance of your Ridgeback spitting it out, and almost none of him refusing it!

Liquid medication can be a bit more difficult to administer, but as with pills or capsules, it can be mixed into your Ridgeback's regular meals. Since you are adding water to his dinner anyway, the taste of the medication will not be as strong, and rarely will a Ridgeback miss a meal because of a little medicine. However, you can also use a marked syringe to put liquid medicine directly into your Ridgeback's mouth. Holding his mouth closed, with chin tipped up, deliver the medicine smoothly to the back of his mouth between his teeth. Be sure to hold his mouth closed until he has swallowed the entire dosage.

Caring for the Senior Dog

The elderly Ridgeback shows the grace and strength of many years of learning and loving. This inner beauty shines in his wise, white face, measured gait and dignified composure.

Your Ridgeback will remain happy and active for many years, as long as you help to keep him that way.

Continue to exercise and play with your elderly dog, even if the pace is much slower than it once was. Take him for outings to the park and for walks to see things that will spark his interest. Mental stimulation keeps an aging dog feeling young and alert, just as it does for human seniors. Let him tell you what he is able to do happily and easily and what is becoming difficult for him.

A senior dog will probably slow down a bit but will still benefit from physical activity and mental stimulation.

Treat your elderly Ridgeback with the respect and care he deserves after a lifetime of devotion. Pay special attention to your pet's health needs. The older dog is not as active, less tolerant of boisterous children and younger dogs and may have very real physical symptoms of illness. Arthritis may cause pain. Weather extremes are more stressful. Incontinence may cause his hygiene as well as his dignity to suffer. Eyesight and hearing will not be as acute. Your veterinarian can help with all of these problems to make your pet's final years as happy and comfortable as all the previous ones. The immense dignity of the Ridgeback deserves nothing less.

Saying Goodbye

When to let go of your senior citizen is a very personal decision. When age and health problems become overwhelming, you must determine whether or not your Ridgeback is ready to move on, or if he will stay happily with you awhile longer. Your vet can give advice, but the decision is still yours.

Your Happy, Healthy Pet

Your Dog's Name _____

Name on Your Dog's Pedigree (if your dog has one) _____

_____

Where Your Dog Came From _____

_____

Your Dog's Birthday _____

Your Dog's Veterinarian

    Name _____

    Address _____

    Phone Number_____

    Emergency Number_____

Your Dog's Health

    Vaccines

    type _____ date given _____

    type _____ date given _____

    type _____ date given _____

    type _____ date given _____

    Heartworm

    date tested _____ type used_____ start date _____

Your Dog's License Number_____

Groomer's Name and Number _____

Dogsitter/Walker's Name and Number_____

Awards Your Dog Has Won

    Award _____ date earned _____

    Award _____ date earned _____

part three

Enjoying
your
Dog

chapter 8

Basic
Training

by Ian Dunbar, Ph.D., MRCVS

Training is the jewel in the crown—the most important aspect of doggy husbandry. There is no more important variable influencing dog behavior and temperament than the dog's education: A well-trained, well-behaved and good-natured puppydog is always a joy to live with, but an untrained and uncivilized dog can be a perpetual nightmare. Moreover, deny the dog an education and it will not have the opportunity to fulfill its own canine potential; neither will it have the ability to communicate effectively with its human companions.

Luckily, modern psychological training methods are easy, efficient and effective and, above all, considerably dog-friendly and user-friendly. Doggy education is as simple as it is enjoyable. But before you can have a good time play-training with your new dog, you have to learn what to do and how to do it. There is no bigger variable influencing the success of dog training than the *owner's* experience and expertise. *Before you embark on the dog's education, you must first educate yourself.*

Basic Training for Owners

Ideally, basic owner training should begin well *before* you select your dog. Find out all you can about your chosen breed first, then master rudimentary training and handling skills. If you already have your puppy/dog, owner training is a dire emergency—the clock is running! Especially for puppies, the first few weeks at home are the most important and influential days in the dog's life. Indeed, the cause of most adolescent and adult problems may be traced back to the initial days the pup explores his new home. This is the time to establish the *status quo*—to teach the puppy/dog how you would like him to behave and so prevent otherwise quite predictable problems.

In addition to consulting breeders and breed books such as this one (which understandably have a positive breed bias), seek out as many pet owners with your breed you can find. Good points are obvious. What you want to find out are the breed-specific *problems,* so you can nip them in the bud. In particular, you should talk to owners with *adolescent* dogs and make a list of all anticipated problems. Most important, *test drive* at least half a dozen adolescent and adult dogs of your breed yourself. An eight-week-old puppy is deceptively easy to handle, but she will acquire adult size, speed and strength in just four months, so you should learn now what to prepare for.

Puppy and pet dog training classes offer a convenient venue to locate pet owners and observe dogs in action. For a list of suitable trainers in your area, contact the Association of Pet Dog Trainers (see Chapter 13). You may also begin your basic owner training by observing other owners in class. Watch as many classes and test drive as many dogs as possible. Select an upbeat, dog-friendly, people-friendly, fun-and-games, puppydog pet training class to learn the ropes. Also, watch training videos and read training books (see Chapter 12). You must find out what to do and how to do it *before* you have to do it.

Principles of Training

Most people think training comprises teaching the dog to do things such as sit, speak and roll over, but even a four-week-old pup knows how to do these things already. Instead, the first step in training involves teaching the dog human words for each dog behavior and activity and for each aspect of the dog's environment. That way you, the owner, can more easily participate in the dog's domestic education by directing him to perform specific actions appropriately, that is, at the right time, in the right place, and so on. Training opens communication channels, enabling an educated dog to at least understand the owner's requests.

In addition to teaching a dog *what* we want her to do, it is also necessary to teach her *why* she should do what we ask. Indeed, 95 percent of training revolves around motivating the dog *to want to do* what we want. Dogs often understand what their owners want; they just don't see the point of doing it—especially when the owner's repetitively boring and seemingly senseless instructions are totally at odds with much more pressing and exciting doggy distractions. It is not so much the dog who is being stubborn or dominant; rather, it is the owner who has failed to acknowledge the dog's needs and feelings and to approach training from the dog's point of view.

The Meaning of Instructions

The secret to successful training is learning how to use training lures to predict or prompt specific behaviors—to coax the dog to do what you want *when* you want. Any highly valued object (such as a treat or toy) may be used as a lure, which the dog will follow with his eyes and nose. Moving the lure in specific ways entices the dog to move his nose, head and entire body in specific ways. In fact, by learning the art of manipulating various lures, it is possible to teach the dog to assume virtually any body position and perform any action. Once you have control over the expression of the dog's behaviors and can elicit any body position or behavior at will, you can easily teach the dog to perform on request.

Tell your dog what you want him to do, use a lure to entice him to respond correctly, then profusely praise

Teach your dog words for each activity he needs to know, like down.

and maybe reward him once he performs the desired action. For example, verbally request "Fido, sit!" while you move a squeaky toy upwards and backwards over the dog's muzzle (lure-movement and hand signal), smile knowingly as he looks up (to follow the lure) and sits down (as a result of canine anatomical engineering), then praise him to distraction ("Gooood Fido!"). Squeak the toy, offer a training treat and give your dog and yourself a pat on the back.

Being able to elicit desired responses over and over enables the owner to reward the dog over and over. Consequently, the dog begins to think training is fun. For example, the more the dog is rewarded for sitting, the more she enjoys sitting. Eventually the dog comes to realize that, whereas most sitting is appreciated, sitting immediately upon request usually prompts especially enthusiastic praise and a slew of high-level rewards. The dog begins to sit on cue much of the time, showing that she is starting to grasp the meaning of the owner's verbal request and hand signal.

Why Comply?

Most dogs enjoy initial lure/reward training and are only too happy to comply with their owners' wishes. Unfortunately, repetitive drilling without appreciative feedback tends to diminish the dog's enthusiasm until he eventually fails to see the point of complying anymore. Moreover, as the dog approaches adolescence he becomes more easily distracted as he develops other interests. Lengthy sessions with repetitive exercises tend to bore and demotivate both parties. If it's not fun, the owner doesn't do it and neither does the dog.

Integrate training into your dog's life: The greater number of training sessions each day and the *shorter* they are, the more willingly compliant your dog will become. Make sure to have a short (just a few seconds) training interlude before every enjoyable canine activity. For example, ask your dog to sit to greet people, to sit before you throw his Frisbee, and to sit for his supper. Really, sitting is no different from a canine "please." Also, include numerous short training interludes during every enjoyable canine pastime, for example, when playing with the dog or when he is running in the park. In this fashion, doggy distractions may be effectively converted into rewards for training. Just as all games have rules, fun becomes training . . . and training becomes fun.

Eventually, rewards actually become unnecessary to continue motivating your dog. If trained with consideration and kindness, performing the desired behaviors will become self-rewarding and, in a sense, your dog will motivate himself. Just as it is not necessary to reward a human companion during an enjoyable walk in the park, or following a game of tennis, it is hardly necessary to reward our best friend—the dog—for walking by our side or while playing fetch. Human

company during enjoyable activities is reward enough for most dogs.

Even though your dog has become self-motivating, it's still good to praise and pet him a lot and offer rewards once in a while, especially for a good job well done. And if for no other reason, praising and rewarding others is good for the human heart.

To train your dog, you need gentle hands, a loving heart and a good attitude.

Punishment

Without a doubt, lure/reward training is by far the best way to teach: Entice your dog to do what you want and then reward him for doing so. Unfortunately, a human shortcoming is to take the good for granted and to moan and groan at the bad. Specifically, the dog's many good behaviors are ignored while the owner focuses on punishing the dog for making mistakes. In extreme cases, instruction is *limited* to punishing mistakes made by a trainee dog, child, employee or husband, even though it has been proven punishment training is notoriously inefficient and ineffective and is decidedly unfriendly and combative. It teaches the dog that training is a drag, almost as quickly as it teaches the dog to dislike his trainer. Why treat our best friends like our worst enemies?

Punishment training is also much more laborious and time consuming. Whereas it takes only a finite amount of time to teach a dog what to chew, for example, it takes much, much longer to punish the dog for each and every mistake. Remember, *there is only one right way!* So why not teach that right way from the outset?!

103

To make matters worse, punishment training causes severe lapses in the dog's reliability. Since it is obviously impossible to punish the dog each and every time she misbehaves, the dog quickly learns to distinguish between those times when she must comply (so as to avoid impending punishment) and those times when she need not comply, because punishment is impossible. Such times include when the dog is off leash and only six feet away, when the owner is otherwise engaged (talking to a friend, watching television, taking a shower, tending to the baby or chatting on the telephone), or when the dog is left at home alone.

Instances of misbehavior will be numerous when the owner is away, because even when the dog complied in the owner's looming presence, he did so unwillingly. The dog was forced to act against his will, rather than moulding his will to want to please. Hence, when the owner is absent, not only does the dog know he need not comply, he simply does not want to. Again, the trainee is not a stubborn vindictive beast, but rather the trainer has failed to teach.

Punishment training invariably creates unpredictable Jekyll and Hyde behavior.

Trainer's Tools

Many training books extol the virtues of a vast array of training paraphernalia and electronic and metallic gizmos, most of which are designed for canine restraint, correction and punishment, rather than for actual facilitation of doggy education. In reality, most effective training tools are not found in stores; they come from within ourselves. In addition to a willing dog, all you really need is a functional human brain, gentle hands, a loving heart and a good attitude.

In terms of equipment, all dogs do require a quality buckle collar to sport dog tags and to attach the leash (for safety and to comply with local leash laws). Hollow chewtoys (like Kongs or sterilized longbones) and a dog bed or collapsible crate are a must for housetraining. Three additional tools are required:

1. specific lures (training treats and toys) to predict and prompt specific desired behaviors;

2. rewards (praise, affection, training treats and toys) to reinforce for the dog what a lot of fun it all is; and

3. knowledge—how to convert the dog's favorite activities and games (potential distractions to training) into "life-rewards," which may be employed to facilitate training.

The most powerful of these is *knowledge*. Education is the key! Watch training classes, participate in training classes, watch videos, read books, enjoy playtraining with your dog, and then your dog will say "Please," and your dog will say "Thank you!"

Housetraining

If dogs were left to their own devices, certainly they would chew, dig and bark for entertainment and then no doubt highlight a few areas of their living space with sprinkles of urine, in much the same way we decorate by hanging pictures. Consequently, when we ask a dog to live with us, we must teach him *where* he may dig and perform his toilet duties, *what* he may chew and *when* he may bark. After all, when left at home alone for many hours, we cannot expect the dog to amuse himself by completing crosswords or watching the soaps on TV!

Also, it would be decidedly unfair to keep the house rules a secret from the dog, and then get angry and punish the poor critter for inevitably transgressing rules he did not even know existed. Remember, without adequate education and guidance, the dog will be forced to establish his own rules—doggy rules—that most probably will be at odds with the owner's view of domestic living.

Since most problems develop during the first few days the dog is at home, prospective dog owners must be certain they are quite clear about the principles of housetraining *before* they get a dog. Early misbehaviors quickly become established as the status quo—

becoming firmly entrenched as hard-to-break bad habits, which set the precedent for years to come. Make sure to teach your dog good habits right from the start. Good habits are just as hard to break as bad ones!

Ideally, when a new dog comes home, try to arrange for someone to be present for as much as possible during the first few days (for adult dogs) or weeks for puppies. With only a little forethought, it is surprisingly easy to find a puppy sitter, such as a retired person, who would be willing to eat from your refrigerator and watch your television while keeping an eye on the newcomer to encourage the dog to play with chewtoys and to ensure he goes outside on a regular basis.

POTTY TRAINING

To teach the dog where to relieve himself:

1. never let him make a single mistake;

2. let him know where you want him to go; and

3. handsomely reward him for doing so:
   "GOOOOOOOD DOG!!!" liver treat, liver treat, liver treat!

PREVENTING MISTAKES

A single mistake is a training disaster, since it heralds many more in future weeks. And each time the dog soils the house, this further reinforces the dog's unfortunate preference for an indoor, carpeted toilet. *Do not let an unhousetrained dog have full run of the house if you are away from home or cannot pay full attention.* Instead, confine the dog to an area where elimination is appropriate, such as an outdoor run or, better still, a small, comfortable indoor kennel with access to an outdoor run. When confined in this manner, most dogs will naturally housetrain themselves.

If that's not possible, confine the dog to an area, such as a utility room, kitchen, basement or garage, where elimination may not be desired in the long run but as an interim measure it is certainly preferable to doing it all around the house. Use newspaper to cover the floor of the dog's day room. The newspaper may be used to soak up the urine and to wrap up and dispose of the feces. Once your dog develops a preferred spot for eliminating, it is only necessary to cover that part of the floor with newspaper. The smaller papered area may then be moved (only a little each day) towards the door to the outside. Thus the dog will develop the tendency to go to the door when he needs to relieve himself.

Never confine an unhousetrained dog to a crate for long periods. Doing so would force the dog to soil the crate and ruin its usefulness as an aid for housetraining (see the following discussion).

The first few weeks at home are the most important and influential in your dog's life.

TEACHING WHERE

In order to teach your dog where you would like her to do her business, you have to be there to direct the proceedings—an obvious, yet often neglected, fact of life. In order to be there to teach the dog *where* to go, you need to know *when* she needs to go. Indeed, the success of housetraining depends on the owner's ability to predict these times. Certainly, a regular feeding schedule will facilitate prediction somewhat, but there is

nothing like "loading the deck" and influencing the timing of the outcome yourself!

Whenever you are at home, make sure the dog is under constant supervision and/or confined to a small area. If already well trained, simply instruct the dog to lie down in his bed or basket. Alternatively, confine the dog to a crate (doggy den) or tie-down (a short, 18-inch lead that can be clipped to an eye hook in the baseboard). Short-term close confinement strongly inhibits urination and defecation, since the dog does not want to soil his sleeping area. Thus, when you release the puppydog each hour, he will definitely need to urinate immediately and defecate every third or fourth hour. Keep the dog confined to his doggy den and take him to his intended toilet area each hour, every hour, and on the hour.

When taking your dog outside, instruct him to sit quietly before opening the door—he will soon learn to sit by the door when he needs to go out!

TEACHING WHY

Being able to predict when the dog needs to go enables the owner to be on the spot to praise and reward the dog. Each hour, hurry the dog to the intended toilet area in the yard, issue the appropriate instruction ("Go pee!" or "Go poop!"), then give the dog three to four minutes to produce. Praise and offer a couple of training treats when successful. The treats are important because many people fail to praise their dogs with feeling . . . and housetraining is hardly the time for understatement. So either loosen up and enthusiastically praise that dog: "Wuzzzer-wuzzer-wuzzer, hoooser good wuffer den? Hoooo went pee for Daddy?" Or say "Good dog!" as best you can and offer the treats for effect.

Following elimination is an ideal time for a spot of playtraining in the yard or house. Also, an empty dog may be allowed greater freedom around the house for the next half hour or so, just as long as you keep an eye out to make sure he does not get into other kinds of mischief. If you are preoccupied and cannot pay full attention, confine the dog to his doggy den once more to enjoy a peaceful snooze or to play with his many chewtoys.

If your dog does not eliminate within the allotted time outside—no biggie! Back to his doggy den, and then try again after another hour.

As I own large dogs, I always feel more relaxed walking an empty dog, knowing that I will not need to finish our stroll weighted down with bags of feces! Beware of falling into the trap of walking the dog to get it to eliminate. The good ol' dog walk is such an enormous highlight in the dog's life that it represents the single biggest potential reward in domestic dogdom. However, when in a hurry, or during inclement weather, many owners abruptly terminate the walk the moment the dog has done its business. This, in effect, severely punishes the dog for doing the right thing, in the right place at the right time. Consequently, many dogs become strongly inhibited from eliminating outdoors because they know it will signal an abrupt end to an otherwise thoroughly enjoyable walk.

Instead, instruct the dog to relieve himself in the yard prior to going for a walk. If you follow the above instructions, most dogs soon learn to eliminate on cue. As soon as the dog eliminates, praise (and offer a treat or two)—"Good dog! Let's go walkies!" Use the walk as a reward for eliminating in the yard. If the dog does not go, put him back in his doggy den and think about a walk later on. You will find with a "No feces–no walk" policy, your dog will become one of the fastest defecators in the business.

If you do not have a back yard, instruct the dog to eliminate right outside your front door prior to the walk. Not only will this facilitate clean up and disposal of the feces in your own trash can but, also, the walk may again be used as a colossal reward.

CHEWING AND BARKING

Short-term close confinement also teaches the dog that occasional quiet moments are a reality of domestic living. Your puppydog is extremely impressionable during his first few weeks at home. Regular confinement at this time soon exerts a calming influence over the dog's personality. Remember, once the dog is housetrained and calmer, there will be a whole lifetime ahead for the dog to enjoy full run of the house and garden. On the other hand, by letting the newcomer have unrestricted access to the entire household and allowing him to run willy-nilly, he will most certainly develop a bunch of behavior problems in short order, no doubt necessitating confinement later in life. It would not be fair to remedially restrain and confine a dog you have trained, through neglect, to run free.

When confining the dog, make sure he always has an impressive array of suitable chewtoys. Kongs and sterilized longbones (both readily available from pet stores) make the best chewtoys, since they are hollow and may be stuffed with treats to heighten the dog's interest. For example, by stuffing the little hole at the top of a Kong with a small piece of freeze-dried liver, the dog will not want to leave it alone.

Remember, treats do not have to be junk food and they certainly should not represent extra calories. Rather, treats should be part of each dog's regular daily diet:

Make sure your puppy has suitable chewtoys.

Some food may be served in the dog's bowl for breakfast and dinner, some food may be used as training treats, and some food may be used for stuffing chewtoys. I regularly stuff my dogs' many Kongs with different shaped biscuits and kibble. The kibble seems to fall out fairly easily, as do the oval-shaped biscuits, thus rewarding the dog instantaneously for checking out the chewtoys. The bone-shaped biscuits fall out after a while, rewarding the dog for worrying at the chewtoy. But the triangular biscuits never come out. They remain inside the Kong as lures, maintaining the dog's fascination with its chewtoy. To further focus the dog's interest, I always make sure to flavor the triangular biscuits by rubbing them with a little cheese or freeze-dried liver.

If stuffed chewtoys are reserved especially for times the dog is confined, the puppy-dog will soon learn to enjoy quiet moments in her doggy den and she will quickly develop a chewtoy habit—a good habit! This is a simple *passive training* process; all the owner has to do is set up the situation and the dog all but trains herself—easy and effective. Even when the dog is given run of the house, her first inclination will be to indulge her rewarding chewtoy habit rather than destroying less-attractive household articles, such as curtains, carpets, chairs and compact disks. Similarly, a chewtoy chewer will be less inclined to scratch and chew herself excessively. Also, if the dog busies herself as a recreational chewer, she will be less inclined to develop into a recreational barker or digger when left at home alone.

Stuff a number of chewtoys whenever the dog is left confined and remove the extra-special-tasting treats when you return. Your dog will now amuse himself with his chewtoys before falling asleep and then resume playing with his chewtoys when he expects you to return. Since most owner-absent misbehavior happens right after you leave and right before your expected return, your puppydog will now be conveniently preoccupied with his chewtoys at these times.

To teach come, call your dog, open your arms as a welcoming signal, wave a toy or a treat and praise for every step in your direction.

Come and Sit

Most puppies will happily approach virtually anyone, whether called or not; that is, until they collide with adolescence and develop other more important doggy interests, such as sniffing a multiplicity of exquisite odors on the grass. Your mission, Mr. and/or Ms. Owner, is to teach and reward the pup for coming reliably, willingly and happily when called—and you have just three months to get it done. Unless adequately reinforced, your puppy's tendency to approach people will self-destruct by adolescence.

Call your dog ("Fido, come!"), open your arms (and maybe squat down) as a welcoming signal, waggle a treat or toy as a lure, and reward the puppydog when he comes running. Do not wait to praise the dog until he reaches you—he may come 95 percent of the way and then run off after some distraction. Instead, praise the dog's *first* step towards you and continue praising enthusiastically for *every* step he takes in your direction.

When the rapidly approaching puppy dog is three lengths away from impact, instruct him to sit ("Fido, sit!") and hold the lure in front of you in an outstretched hand to prevent him from hitting you midchest and knocking you flat on your back! As Fido decelerates to nose the lure, move the treat upwards and backwards just over his muzzle with an upwards motion of your extended arm (palm-upwards). As the dog looks up to follow the lure, he will sit down (if he jumps up, you are holding the lure too high). Praise the dog for sitting. Move backwards and call him again. Repeat this many times over, always praising when Fido comes and sits; on occasion, reward him.

For the first couple of trials, use a training treat both as a lure to entice the dog to come and sit and as a reward for doing so. Thereafter, try to use different items as lures and rewards. For example, lure the dog with a Kong or Frisbee but reward her with a food treat. Or lure the dog with a food treat but pat her and throw a tennis ball as a reward. After just a few repetitions, dispense with the lures and rewards; the dog will begin to respond willingly to your verbal requests and hand signals just for the prospect of praise from your heart and affection from your hands.

Instruct every family member, friend and visitor how to get the dog to come and sit. Invite people over for a series of pooch parties; do not keep the pup a secret— let other people enjoy this puppy, and let the pup enjoy other people. Puppydog parties are not only fun, they easily attract a lot of people to help *you* train *your* dog. Unless you teach your dog *how* to meet people, that is, to sit for greetings, no doubt the dog will resort to jumping up. Then you and the visitors will get annoyed, and the dog will be punished. This is not fair. *Send out those invitations for puppy parties and teach your dog to be mannerly and socially acceptable.*

Even though your dog quickly masters obedient recalls in the house, his reliability may falter when playing in the back yard or local park. Ironically, it is *the owner* who has unintentionally trained the dog *not* to respond in these instances. By allowing the dog to play and run around and otherwise have a good time, but then to call the dog to put him on leash to take him home, the dog quickly learns playing is fun but training is a drag. Thus, playing in the park becomes a severe distraction, which works against training. Bad news!

Instead, whether playing with the dog off leash or on leash, request him to come at frequent intervals— say, every minute or so. On most occasions, praise and pet the dog for a few seconds while he is sitting, then tell him to go play again. For especially fast recalls, offer a couple of training treats and take the time to praise and pet the dog enthusiastically before releasing him. The dog will learn that coming when called is not necessarily the end of the play session, and neither is it the end of the world; rather, it signals an enjoyable, quality time-out with the owner before resuming play once more. In fact, playing in the park now becomes a very effective life-reward, which works to facilitate training by reinforcing each obedient and timely recall. Good news!

Sit, Down, Stand and Rollover

Teaching the dog a variety of body positions is easy for owner and dog, impressive for spectators and extremely useful for all. Using lure-reward techniques, it is possible to train several positions at once to verbal commands or hand signals (which impress the socks off onlookers).

Sit and ***down***—the two control commands—prevent or resolve nearly a hundred behavior problems. For example, if the dog happily and obediently sits or lies down when requested, he cannot jump on visitors, dash out the front door, run around and chase its tail, pester other dogs, harass cats or annoy family, friends or strangers. Additionally, "sit" or "down" are better emergency commands for off-leash control.

It is easier to teach and maintain a reliable sit than maintain a reliable recall. *Sit* is the purest and simplest of commands—either the dog is sitting or he is not. If there is any change of circumstances or potential danger in the park, for example, simply instruct the dog to sit. If he sits, you have a number of options: allow the dog to resume playing when he is safe; walk up and put the dog on leash, or call the dog. The dog will be much more likely to come when called if he has already acknowledged his compliance by sitting. If the dog does not sit in the park—train him to!

Stand and ***rollover-stay*** are the two positions for examining the dog. Your veterinarian will love you to distraction if you take a little time to teach the dog to stand still and roll over and play possum. Also, your vet bills will be smaller. The rollover-stay is an especially useful command and is really just a variation of the down-stay: whereas the dog lies prone in the traditional down, she lies supine in the rollover-stay.

As with teaching come and sit, the training techniques to teach the dog to assume all other body positions on cue are user-friendly and dog-friendly. Simply give the appropriate request, lure the dog into the desired body position using a training treat or toy and then *praise* (and maybe reward) the dog as soon as he complies. Try not to touch the dog to get him to respond. If you teach the dog by guiding him into position, the dog will quickly learn that rump-pressure means sit, for example, but as yet you still have no control over your dog if he is just six feet away. It will still be necessary to teach the dog to sit on request. So do not make training a time-consuming two-step process; instead, teach the dog to sit to a verbal request or hand signal from the outset. Once the dog sits willingly when requested, by all means use your hands to pet the dog when he does so.

To teach *down* when the dog is already sitting, say "Fido, down!," hold the lure in one hand (palm down) and lower that hand to the floor between the dog's forepaws. As the dog lowers his head to follow the lure, slowly move the lure away from the dog just a fraction (in front of his paws). The dog will lie down as he stretches his nose forward to follow the lure. Praise the dog when he does so. If the dog stands up, you pulled the lure away too far and too quickly.

When teaching the dog to lie down from the standing position, say "down" and lower the lure to the floor as before. Once the dog has lowered his forequarters and assumed a play bow, gently and slowly move the lure *towards* the dog between his forelegs. Praise the dog as soon as his rear end plops down.

After just a couple of trials it will be possible to alternate sits and downs and have the dog energetically perform doggy push-ups. Praise the dog a lot, and after half a dozen or so push-ups reward the dog with a training treat or toy. You will notice the more energetically you move your arm—upwards (palm up) to get the dog to sit, and downwards (palm down) to get the dog to lie down—the more energetically the dog responds to your requests. Now try training the dog in silence and you will notice he has also learned to respond to hand signals. Yeah! Not too shabby for the first session.

To teach *stand* from the sitting position, say "Fido, stand," slowly move the lure half a dog-length away from the dog's nose, keeping it at nose level, and praise the dog as he stands to follow the lure. As soon

Using a food lure to teach sit, down and stand. 1) "Phoenix, Sit." 2) Hand palm upwards, move lure up and back over dog's muzzle. 3) "Good sit, Phoenix!" 4) "Phoenix, down." 5) Hand palm downwards, move lure down to lie between dog's forepaws. 6) "Phoenix, off. Good down, Phoenix!" 7) "Phoenix, sit!" 8) Palm upwards, move lure up and back, keeping it close to dog's muzzle. 9) "Good sit, Phoenix!"

10) "Phoenix, stand!" 11) Move lure away from dog at nose height, then lower it a tad. 12) "Phoenix, off! Good stand, Phoenix!" 13) "Phoenix, down!" 14) Hand palm downwards, move lure down to lie between dog's forepaws. 15) "Phoenix, off! Good down-stay, Phoenix!" 16) "Phoenix, stand!" 17) Move lure away from dog's muzzle up to nose height. 18) "Phoenix,off! Good stand-stay, Phoenix. Now we'll make the vet and groomer happy!"

as the dog stands, lower the lure to just beneath the dog's chin to entice him to look down; otherwise he will stand and then sit immediately. To prompt the dog to stand from the down position, move the lure half a dog-length upwards and away from the dog, holding the lure at standing nose height from the floor.

Teaching **rollover** is best started from the down position, with the dog lying on one side, or at least with both hind legs stretched out on the same side. Say "Fido, bang!" and move the lure backwards and alongside the dog's muzzle to its elbow (on the side of its outstretched hind legs). Once the dog looks to the side and backwards, very slowly move the lure upwards to the dog's shoulder and backbone. Tickling the dog in the goolies (groin area) often invokes a reflex-raising of the hind leg as an appeasement gesture, which facilitates the tendency to roll over. If you move the lure too quickly and the dog jumps into the standing position, have patience and start again. As soon as the dog rolls onto its back, keep the lure stationary and mesmerize the dog with a relaxing tummy rub.

To teach **rollover-stay** when the dog is standing or moving, say "Fido, bang!" and give the appropriate hand signal (with index finger pointed and thumb cocked in true Sam Spade fashion), then in one fluid movement lure him to first lie down and then rollover-stay as above.

Teaching the dog to **stay** in each of the above four positions becomes a piece of cake after first teaching the dog not to worry at the toy or treat training lure. This is best accomplished by hand feeding dinner kibble. Hold a piece of kibble firmly in your hand and softly instruct "Off!" Ignore any licking and slobbering *for however long the dog worries at the treat,* but say "Take it!" and offer the kibble *the instant* the dog breaks contact with his muzzle. Repeat this a few times, and then up the ante and insist the dog remove his muzzle for one whole second before offering the kibble. Then progressively refine your criteria and have the dog not touch your hand (or treat) for longer and longer periods on each trial, such as for two seconds, four seconds, then six, ten, fifteen, twenty, thirty seconds and so on. The dog soon learns: (1) worrying at the treat never gets results, whereas (2) noncontact is often rewarded after a variable time lapse.

Teaching *"Off!"* has many useful applications in its own right. Additionally, instructing the dog not to touch a training lure often produces spontaneous and magical stays. Request the dog to stand-stay, for example, and not to touch the lure. At first set your sights on a short two-second stay before rewarding the dog. (Remember, every long journey begins with a single step.) However, on subsequent trials, gradually and progressively increase the length of stay required to receive a reward. In no time at all your dog will stand calmly for a minute or so.

Relevancy Training

Once you have taught the dog what you expect her to do when requested to come, sit, lie down, stand, rollover and stay, the time is right to teach the dog *why* she should comply with your wishes. The secret is to have many (*many*) extremely short training interludes (two to five seconds each) at numerous (*numerous*) times during the course of the dog's day. Especially work with the dog immediately *before* the dog's good times and *during* the dog's good times. For example, ask your dog to sit and/or lie down each time before opening doors, serving meals, offering treats and tummy rubs; ask the dog to perform a few controlled doggy push-ups before letting her off-leash or throwing a tennis ball; and perhaps request the dog to sit-down-sit-stand-down-stand-rollover before inviting her to cuddle on the couch.

Similarly, request the dog to sit many times during play or on walks, and in no time at all the dog will be only too pleased to follow your instructions because he has learned that a compliant response heralds all sorts of goodies. Basically all you are trying to teach the dog is how to say please: "Please throw the tennis ball. Please may I snuggle on the couch."

Remember, whereas it is important to keep training interludes short, it is equally important to have many short sessions each and every day. The shortest (and most useful) session comprises asking the dog to sit and then go play during a play session. When trained this way, your dog will soon associate training with good times. In fact, the dog may be unable to distinguish between training and good times and, indeed, there should be no distinction. The warped concept that training involves forcing the dog to comply and/or dominating his will is totally at odds with the picture of a truly well-trained dog. In reality, enjoying a game of training with a dog is no different from enjoying a game of backgammon or tennis with a friend; and walking with a dog should be no different from strolling with buddies on the golf course.

Walk by Your Side

Many people attempt to teach a dog to heel by putting him on a leash and physically correcting the dog when he makes mistakes. There are a number of things seriously wrong with this approach, the first being that most people do not want precision heeling; rather, they simply want the dog to follow or walk by their side. Second, when physically restrained during "training," even though the dog may grudgingly mope by your side when "handcuffed" on leash, let's see what happens when he is off leash. History! The dog is in the next county because he never enjoyed walking with you on leash and you have no control over him off leash. So let's just teach the dog off leash from the outset to *want* to walk with us. Third, if the dog has not been trained to heel, it is a trifle hasty to think about punishing the poor dog for making mistakes and breaking heeling rules he didn't even know existed. This is simply not fair! Surely, if the dog had been adequately taught how to heel, he would seldom make mistakes and hence there would be no need to correct the dog. Remember, each mistake and each correction (punishment) advertise the trainer's inadequacy, not the dog's. The dog is not stubborn, he is not stupid and he is not bad. Even if he were, he would still require training, so let's train him properly.

Let's teach the dog to *enjoy* following us and to *want* to walk by our side offleash. Then it will be easier to teach high-precision off-leash heeling patterns if desired. After attaching the leash for safety on outdoor walks, but before going anywhere, it is necessary to teach the dog specifically not to pull. Now it will be much easier to teach on-leash walking and heeling because the dog already wants to walk with you, he is familiar with the desired walking and heeling positions and he knows not to pull.

FOLLOWING

Start by training your dog to follow you. Many puppies will follow if you simply walk away from them and maybe click your fingers or chuckle. Adult dogs may require additional enticement to stimulate them to follow, such as a training lure or, at the very least, a lively trainer. To teach the dog to follow: (1) keep walking and (2) walk away from the dog. If the dog attempts to lead or lag, change pace; slow down if the dog forges too far ahead, but speed up if he lags too far behind. Say "Steady!" or "Easy!" each time before you slow down and "Quickly!" or "Hustle!" each time before you speed up, and the dog will learn to change pace on cue. If the dog lags or leads too far, or if he wanders right or left, simply walk quickly in the opposite direction and maybe even run away from the dog and hide.

Practicing is a lot of fun; you can set up a course in your home, yard or park to do this. Indoors, entice the dog to follow upstairs, into a bedroom, into the bathroom, downstairs, around the living room couch, zigzagging between dining room chairs and into the kitchen for dinner. Outdoors, get the dog to follow around park benches, trees, shrubs and along walkways and lines in the grass. (For safety outdoors, it is advisable to attach a long line on the dog, but never exert corrective tension on the line.)

Remember, following has a lot to do with attitude—*your* attitude! Most probably your dog will *not* want to follow Mr. Grumpy Troll with the personality of wilted lettuce. Lighten up—walk with a jaunty step, whistle a happy tune, sing, skip and tell jokes to your dog and he will be right there by your side.

BY YOUR SIDE

It is smart to train the dog to walk close on one side or the other—either side will do, your choice. When walking, jogging or cycling, it is generally bad news to have the dog suddenly cut in front of you. In fact, I train my dogs to walk "By my side" and "Other side"—both very useful instructions. It is possible to position the dog fairly accurately by looking to the appropriate side and clicking your fingers or slapping your thigh on that side. A precise positioning may be attained by holding a training lure, such as a chewtoy, tennis ball, or food treat. Stop and stand still several times throughout the walk, just as you would when window shopping or meeting a friend. Use the lure to make sure the dog slows down and stays close whenever you stop.

When teaching the dog to heel, we generally want her to sit in heel position when we stop. Teach heel

Using a toy to teach sit-heel-sit sequences: 1) "Phoenix, heel!" Standing still, move lure up and back over dog's muzzle.... 2) To position dog sitting in heel position on your left side. 3) "Phoenix, heel!" wagging lure in left hand. Change lure to right hand in preparation for sit signal.

position at the standstill and the dog will learn that the default heel position is sitting by your side (left or right—your choice, unless you wish to compete in obedience trials, in which case the dog must heel on the left).

Several times a day, stand up and call your dog to come and sit in heel position—"Fido, heel!" For example, instruct the dog to come to heel each time there are commercials on TV, or each time you turn a page of a novel, and the dog will get it in a single evening.

Practice straight-line heeling and turns separately. With the dog sitting at heel, teach him to turn in place. After each quarter-turn, half-turn or full turn in place, lure the dog to sit at heel. Now it's time for short straight-line heeling sequences, no more than a few steps at a time. Always think of heeling in terms of Sit-Heel-Sit sequences—start and end with the dog in position and do your best to keep him there when moving. Progressively increase the number of steps in each sequence. When the dog remains close for 20 yards of straight-line heeling, it is time to add a few turns and then sign up for a happy-heeling obedience class to get some advice from the experts.

4) Use hand signal only to lure dog to sit as you stop. Eventually, dog will sit automatically at heel whenever you stop. 5) "Good dog!"

No Pulling on Leash

You can start teaching your dog not to pull on leash anywhere—in front of the television or outdoors—but regardless of location, you must not take a single step with tension in the leash. For a reason known only to dogs, even just a couple of paces of pulling on leash is intrinsically motivating and diabolically rewarding. Instead, attach the leash to the dog's collar, grasp the other end firmly with both hands held close to your chest, and stand still—do not budge an inch. Have somebody watch you with a stopwatch to time your progress, or else you will never believe this will work and so you will not even try the exercise, and your shoulder and the dog's neck will be traumatized for years to come.

Stand still and wait for the dog to stop pulling, and to sit and/or lie down. All dogs stop pulling and sit eventually. Most take only a couple of minutes; the all-time record is 22 ⅕ minutes. Time how long it takes. Gently praise the dog when he stops pulling, and as soon as he sits, enthusiastically praise the dog and take just one step forwards, then immediately stand still. This single step usually demonstrates the ballistic reinforcing nature of pulling on leash; most dogs explode to the end of the leash, so be prepared for the strain. Stand firm and wait for the dog to sit again. Repeat this half a dozen times and you will probably notice a progressive reduction in the force of the dog's one-step explosions and a radical reduction in the time it takes for the dog to sit each time.

As the dog learns "Sit we go" and "Pull we stop," she will begin to walk forward calmly with each single step and automatically sit when you stop. Now try two steps before you stop. Wooooooo! Scary! When the dog has mastered two steps at a time, try for three. After each success, progressively increase the number of steps in the sequence: try four steps and then six, eight, ten and twenty steps before stopping. Congratulations! You are now walking the dog on leash.

Whenever walking with the dog (off leash or on leash), make sure you stop periodically to practice a few position commands and stays before instructing the dog to "Walk on!" (Remember, you want the dog to be compliant everywhere, not just in the kitchen when his dinner is at hand.) For example, stopping every 25 yards to briefly train the dog amounts to over 200 training interludes within a single three-mile stroll. And each training session is in a different location. You will not believe the improvement within just the first mile of the first walk.

To put it another way, integrating training into a walk offers 200 separate opportunities to use the continuance of the walk as a reward to reinforce the dog's education. Moreover, some training interludes may comprise continuing education for the dog's walking skills: Alternate short periods of the dog walking calmly by your side with periods when the dog is allowed to sniff and investigate the environment. Now sniffing odors on the grass and meeting other dogs become rewards which reinforce the dog's calm and mannerly demeanor. Good Lord! Whatever next? Many enjoyable walks together of course. Happy trails!

THE IMPORTANCE OF TRICKS

Nothing will improve a dog's quality of life better than having a few tricks under its belt. Teaching any trick expands the dog's vocabulary, which facilitates communication and improves the owner's control. Also, specific tricks help prevent and resolve specific behavior problems. For example, by teaching the dog to fetch his toys, the dog learns carrying a toy makes the owner happy and, therefore, will be more likely to chew his toy than other inappropriate items.

More important, teaching tricks prompts owners to lighten up and train with a sunny disposition. Really, tricks should be no different from any other behaviors we put on cue. But they are. When teaching tricks, owners have a much sweeter attitude, which in turn motivates the dog and improves her willingness to comply. The dog feels tricks are a blast, but formal commands are a drag. In fact, tricks are so enjoyable, they may be used as rewards in training by asking the dog to come, sit and down-stay and then rollover for a tummy rub. Go on, try it: Crack a smile and even giggle when the dog promptly and willingly lies down and stays.

Most important, performing tricks prompts onlookers to smile and giggle. Many people are scared of dogs, especially large ones. And nothing can be more off-putting for a dog than to be constantly confronted by strangers who don't like him because of his size or the way he looks. Uneasy people put the dog on edge, causing him to back off and bark, only frightening people all the more. And so a vicious circle develops, with the people's fear fueling the dog's fear *and vice versa*. Instead, tie a pink ribbon to your dog's collar and practice all sorts of tricks on walks and in the park, and you will be pleasantly amazed how it changes people's attitudes toward your friendly dog. The dog's repertoire of tricks is limited only by the trainer's imagination. Below I have described three of my favorites:

SPEAK AND SHUSH

The training sequence involved in teaching a dog to bark on request is no different from that used when training any behavior on cue: request—lure—response—reward. As always, the secret of success lies in finding an effective lure. If the dog always barks at the doorbell, for example, say "Rover, speak!", have an accomplice ring the doorbell, then reward the dog for barking. After a few woofs, ask Rover to "Shush!", waggle a food treat under his nose (to entice him to sniff and thus to shush), praise him when quiet and eventually offer the treat as a reward. Alternate "Speak" and "Shush," progressively increasing the length of shush-time between each barking bout.

PLAYBOW

With the dog standing, say "Bow!" and lower the food lure (palm upwards) to rest between the dog's forepaws. Praise as the dog lowers her forequarters and sternum to the ground (as when teaching the down), but then lure the dog to stand and offer the treat. On successive trials, gradually increase the length of time the dog is required to remain in the playbow posture in order to gain a food reward. If the dog's rear end collapses into a down, say nothing and offer no reward; simply start over.

BE A BEAR

With the dog sitting backed into a corner to prevent him from toppling over backwards, say "Be a Bear!" With bent paw and palm down, raise a lure upwards and backwards along the top of the dog's muzzle. Praise the dog when he sits up on his haunches and offer the treat as a reward. To prevent the dog from standing on his hind legs, keep the lure closer to the dog's muzzle. On each trial, progressively increase the length of time the dog is required to sit up to receive a food reward. Since lure/ reward training is so easy, teach the dog to stand and walk on his hind legs as well!

Teaching "Be a Bear"

chapter 9

Getting
Active
with your Dog
by Bardi McLennan

Once you and your dog have graduated from basic obedience training and are beginning to work together as a team, you can take part in the growing world of dog activities. There are so many fun things to do with your dog! Just remember, people and dogs don't always learn at the same pace, so don't be upset if you (or your dog) need more than two basic training courses before your team becomes operational. Even smart dogs don't go straight to college from kindergarten!

Just as there are events geared to certain types of dogs, so there are ones that are more appealing to certain types of people. In some activities, you give the commands and your dog does the work (upland game hunting is one example), while in others, such as agility, you'll both get a work-out. You may want to aim for prestigious titles to add to your dog's name, or you may want nothing more than the sheer enjoyment of being around other people and their dogs. Passive or active, participation has its own rewards.

Consider your dog's physical capabilities when looking into any of the canine activities. It's easy to see that a Basset Hound is not built for the racetrack, nor would a Chihuahua be the breed of choice for pulling a sled. A loyal dog will attempt almost anything you ask him to do, so it is up to you to know your

All dogs seem to love playing flyball.

dog's limitations. A dog must be physically sound in order to compete at any level in athletic activities, and being mentally sound is a definite plus. Advanced age, however, may not be a deterrent. Many dogs still hunt and herd at ten or twelve years of age. It's entirely possible for dogs to be "fit at 50." Take your dog for a checkup, explain to your vet the type of activity you have in mind and be guided by his or her findings.

You needn't be restricted to breed-specific sports if it's only fun you're after. Certain AKC activities are limited to designated breeds; however, as each new trial, test or sport has grown in popularity, so has the variety of breeds encouraged to participate at a fun level.

But don't shortchange your fun, or that of your dog, by thinking only of the basic function of her breed. Once a dog has learned how to learn, she can be taught to do just about anything as long as the size of the dog is right for the job and you both think it is fun and rewarding. In other words, you are a team.

To get involved in any of the activities detailed in this chapter, look for the names and addresses of the organizations that sponsor them in Chapter 13. You can also ask your breeder or a local dog trainer for contacts.

You can compete in obedience trials with a well trained dog.

Official American Kennel Club Activities

The following tests and trials are some of the events sanctioned by the AKC and sponsored by various dog clubs. Your dog's expertise will be rewarded with impressive titles. You can participate just for fun, or be competitive and go for those awards.

OBEDIENCE

Training classes begin with pups as young as three months of age in kindergarten puppy training, then advance to pre-novice (all exercises on lead) and go on to novice, which is where you'll start off-lead work. In obedience classes dogs learn to sit, stay, heel and come through a variety of exercises. Once you've got the basics down, you can enter obedience trials and work toward earning your dog's first degree, a C.D. (Companion Dog).

The next level is called "Open," in which jumps and retrieves perk up the dog's interest. Passing grades in competition at this level earn a C.D.X. (Companion Dog Excellent). Beyond that lies the goal of the most ambitious—Utility (U.D. and even U.D.X. or OTCh, an Obedience Champion).

AGILITY

All dogs can participate in the latest canine sport to have gained worldwide popularity for its fun and excitement, agility. It began in England as a canine version of horse show-jumping, but because dogs are more agile and able to perform on verbal commands, extra feats were added such as climbing, balancing and racing through tunnels or in and out of weave poles.

Many of the obstacles (regulation or homemade) can be set up in your own backyard. If the agility bug bites, you could end up in international competition!

For starters, your dog should be obedience trained, even though, in the beginning, the lessons may all be taught on lead. Once the dog understands the commands (and you do, too), it's as easy as guiding the dog over a prescribed course, one obstacle at a time. In competition, the race is against the clock, so wear your running shoes! The dog starts with 200 points and the judge deducts for infractions and misadventures along the way.

All dogs seem to love agility and respond to it as if they were being turned loose in a playground paradise. Your dog's enthusiasm will be contagious; agility turns into great fun for dog and owner.

FIELD TRIALS AND HUNTING TESTS

There are field trials and hunting tests for the sporting breeds—retrievers, spaniels and pointing breeds, and for some hounds—Bassets, Beagles and Dachshunds. Field trials are competitive events that test a dog's ability to perform the functions for which she was bred. Hunting tests, which are open to retrievers,

---

TITLES AWARDED BY THE AKC

Conformation: Ch. (Champion)

Obedience: CD (Companion Dog); CDX (Companion Dog Excellent); UD (Utility Dog); UDX (Utility Dog Excellent); OTCh. (Obedience Trial Champion)

Field: JH (Junior Hunter); SH (Senior Hunter); MH (Master Hunter); AFCh. (Amateur Field Champion); FCh. (Field Champion)

Lure Coursing: JC (Junior Courser); SC (Senior Courser)

Herding: HT (Herding Tested); PT (Pre-Trial Tested); HS (Herding Started); HI (Herding Intermediate); HX (Herding Excellent); HCh. (Herding Champion)

Tracking: TD (Tracking Dog); TDX (Tracking Dog Excellent)

Agility: NAD (Novice Agility); OAD (Open Agility); ADX (Agility Excellent); MAX (Master Agility)

Earthdog Tests: JE (Junior Earthdog); SE (Senior Earthdog); ME (Master Earthdog)

Canine Good Citizen: CGC

Combination: DC (Dual Champion—Ch. and Fch.); TC (Triple Champion—Ch., Fch., and OTCh.)

spaniels and pointing breeds only, are noncompetitive and are a means of judging the dog's ability as well as that of the handler.

Hunting is a very large and complex part of canine sports, and if you own one of the breeds that hunts, the events are a great treat for your dog and you. He gets to do what he was bred for, and you get to work with him and watch him do it. You'll be proud of and amazed at what your dog can do.

Fortunately, the AKC publishes a series of booklets on these events, which outline the rules and regulations and include a glossary of the sometimes complicated terms. The AKC also publishes newsletters for field trialers and hunting test enthusiasts. The United Kennel Club (UKC) also has informative materials for the hunter and his dog.

Retrievers and other sporting breeds get to do what they're bred to in hunting tests.

HERDING TESTS AND TRIALS

Herding, like hunting, dates back to the first known uses man made of dogs. The interest in herding today is widespread, and if you own a herding breed, you can join in the activity. Herding dogs are tested for their natural skills to keep a flock of ducks, sheep or cattle together. If your dog shows potential, you can start at the testing level, where your dog can earn a title for showing an inherent herding ability. With training you can advance to the trial level, where your dog should be capable of controlling even difficult livestock in diverse situations.

LURE COURSING

The AKC Tests and Trials for Lure Coursing are open to traditional sighthounds—Greyhounds, Whippets,

Borzoi, Salukis, Afghan Hounds, Ibizan Hounds and Scottish Deerhounds—as well as to Basenjis and Rhodesian Ridgebacks. Hounds are judged on overall ability, follow, speed, agility and endurance. This is possibly the most exciting of the trials for spectators, because the speed and agility of the dogs is awesome to watch as they chase the lure (or "course") in heats of two or three dogs at a time.

TRACKING

Tracking is another activity in which almost any dog can compete because every dog that sniffs the ground when taken outdoors is, in fact, tracking. The hard part comes when the rules as to what, when and where the dog tracks are determined by a person, not the dog! Tracking tests cover a large area of fields, woods and roads. The tracks are laid hours before the dogs go to work on them, and include "tricks" like cross-tracks and sharp turns. If you're interested in search-and-rescue work, this is the place to start.

This tracking dog is hot on the trail.

EARTHDOG TESTS FOR SMALL TERRIERS AND DACHSHUNDS

These tests are open to Australian, Bedlington, Border, Cairn, Dandie Dinmont, Smooth and Wire Fox, Lakeland, Norfolk, Norwich, Scottish, Sealyham, Skye, Welsh and West Highland White Terriers as well as Dachshunds. The dogs need no prior training for this terrier sport. There is a qualifying test on the day of the event, so dog and handler learn the rules on the spot. These tests, or "digs," sometimes end with informal races in the late afternoon.

Here are some of the extracurricular obedience and racing activities that are not regulated by the AKC or UKC, but are generally run by clubs or a group of dog fanciers and are often open to all.

Canine Freestyle This activity is something new on the scene and is variously likened to dancing, dressage or ice skating. It is meant to show the athleticism of the dog, but also requires showmanship on the part of the dog's handler. If you and your dog like to ham it up for friends, you might want to look into freestyle.

Lure coursing lets sighthounds do what they do best—run!

Scent Hurdle Racing Scent hurdle racing is purely a fun activity sponsored by obedience clubs with members forming competing teams. The height of the hurdles is based on the size of the shortest dog on the team. On a signal, one team dog is released on each of two side-by-side courses and must clear every hurdle before picking up its own dumbbell from a platform and returning over the jumps to the handler. As each dog returns, the next on that team is sent. Of course, that is what the dogs are supposed to do. When the dogs improvise (going under or around the hurdles, stealing another dog's dumbbell, and so forth), it no doubt frustrates the handlers, but just adds to the fun for everyone else.

Flyball This type of racing is similar, but after negotiating the four hurdles, the dog comes to a flyball box, steps on a lever that releases a tennis ball into the air, catches the ball and returns over the hurdles to the starting point. This game also becomes extremely fun for spectators because the dogs sometimes cheat by catching a ball released by the dog in the next lane. Three titles can be earned—Flyball Dog (F.D.), Flyball Dog Excellent (F.D.X.) and Flyball Dog Champion (Fb.D.Ch.)—all awarded by the North American Flyball Association, Inc.

Dogsledding The name conjures up the Rocky Mountains or the frigid North, but you can find dogsled clubs in such unlikely spots as Maryland, North Carolina and Virginia! Dogsledding is primarily for the Nordic breeds such as the Alaskan Malamutes, Siberian Huskies and Samoyeds, but other breeds can try. There are some practical backyard applications to this sport, too. With parental supervision, almost any strong dog could pull a child's sled.

Coming over the A-frame on an agility course.

These are just some of the many recreational ways you can get to know and understand your multifaceted dog better and have fun doing it.

chapter 10

Your Dog
and your
Family

by Bardi McLennan

Adding a dog automatically increases your family by one, no matter whether you live alone in an apartment or are part of a mother, father and six kids household. The single-person family is fair game for numerous and varied canine misconceptions as to who is dog and who pays the bills, whereas a dog in a houseful of children will consider himself to be just one of the gang, littermates all. One dog and one child may give a dog reason to believe they are both kids or both dogs.

Either interpretation requires parental supervision and sometimes speedy intervention.

As soon as one paw goes through the door into your home, Rufus (or Rufina) has to make many adjustments to become a part of your family. Your job is to make him fit in as painlessly as possible. An older dog may have some frame of reference from past experience, but to a 10-week-old puppy, everything is brand new: people, furniture, stairs, when and where people eat, sleep or watch TV, his own place and everyone else's space, smells, sounds, outdoors—everything!

Puppies, and newly acquired dogs of any age, do not need what we think of as "freedom." If you leave a new dog or puppy loose in the house, you will almost certainly return to chaotic destruction and the dog will forever after equate your homecoming with a time of punishment to be dreaded. It is unfair to give your dog what amounts to "freedom to get into trouble." Instead, confine him to a crate for brief periods of your absence (up to three or four hours) and, for the long haul, a workday for example, confine him to one untrashable area with his own toys, a bowl of water and a radio left on (low) in another room.

Lots of pets get along with each other just fine.

For the first few days, when not confined, put Rufus on a long leash tied to your wrist or waist. This umbilical cord method enables the dog to learn all about you from your body language and voice, and to learn by his own actions which things in the house are NO! and which ones are rewarded by "Good dog." House-training will be easier with the pup always by your side. Speaking of which, accidents do happen. That goal of "completely housetrained" takes up to a year, or the length of time it takes the pup to mature.

The All-Adult Family

Most dogs in an adults-only household today are likely to be latchkey pets, with no one home all day but the dog. When you return after a tough day on the job, the dog can and should be your relaxation therapy. But going home can instead be a daily frustration.

Separation anxiety is a very common problem for the dog in a working household. It may begin with whines and barks of loneliness, but it will soon escalate into a frenzied destruction derby. That is why it is so important to set aside the time to teach a dog to relax when left alone in his confined area and to understand that he can trust you to return.

Let the dog get used to your work schedule in easy stages. Confine him to one room and go in and out of that room over and over again. Be casual about it. No physical, voice or eye contact. When the pup no longer even notices your comings and goings, leave the house for varying lengths of time, returning to stay home for a few minutes and gradually increasing the time away. This training can take days, but the dog is learning that you haven't left him forever and that he can trust you.

Any time you leave the dog, but especially during this training period, be casual about your departure. No anxiety-building fond farewells. Just "Bye" and go! Remember the "Good dog" when you return to find everything more or less as you left it.

If things are a mess (or even a disaster) when you return, greet the dog, take him outside to eliminate, and then put him in his crate while you clean up. Rant and rave in the shower! *Do not* punish the dog. You were not there when it happened, and the rule is: Only punish as you catch the dog in the act of wrongdoing. Obviously, it makes sense to get your latchkey puppy when you'll have a week or two to spend on these training essentials.

Family weekend activities should include Rufus whenever possible. Depending on the pup's age, now is the time for a long walk in the park, playtime in the backyard, a hike in the woods. Socializing is as important as health care, good food and physical exercise, so visiting Aunt Emma or Uncle Harry and the next-door neighbor's dog or cat is essential to developing an out-going, friendly temperament in your pet.

If you are a single adult, socializing Rufus at home and away will prevent him from becoming overly protective of you (or just overly attached) and will also prevent such behavioral problems as dominance or fear of strangers.

Babies

Whether already here or on the way, babies figure larger than life in the eyes of a dog. If the dog is there first, let him in on all your baby preparations in the house. When baby arrives, let Rufus sniff any item of clothing that has been on the baby before Junior comes home. Then let Mom greet the dog first before introducing the new family member. Hold the baby down for the dog to see and sniff, but make sure some-

one's holding the dog on lead in case of any sudden moves. Don't play keep-away or tease the dog with the baby, which only invites undesirable jumping up.

The dog and the baby are "family," and for starters can be treated almost as equals. Things rapidly change, however, especially when baby takes to creeping around on all fours on the dog's turf or, better yet, has yummy pudding all over her face and hands! That's when a lot of things in the dog's and baby's lives become more separate than equal.

Dogs are perfect confidants.

Toddlers make terrible dog owners, but if you can't avoid the combination, use patient discipline (that is, positive teaching rather than punishment), and use time-outs before you run out of patience.

A dog and a baby (or toddler, or an assertive young child) should never be left alone together. Take the dog with you or confine him. With a baby or youngsters in the house, you'll have plenty of use for that wonderful canine safety device called a crate!

Young Children

Any dog in a house with kids will behave pretty much as the kids do, good or bad. But even good dogs and good children can get into trouble when play becomes rowdy and active.

Teach children how to play nicely with a puppy.

Legs bobbing up and down, shrill voices screeching, a ball hurtling overhead, all add up to exuberant frustration for a dog who's just trying to be part of the gang. In a pack of puppies, any legs or toys being chased would be caught by a set of teeth, and all the pups involved would understand that is how the game is played. Kids do not understand this, nor do parents tolerate it. Bring Rufus indoors before you have reason to regret it. This is time-out, not a punishment.

You can explain the situation to the children and tell them they must play quieter games until the puppy learns not to grab them with his mouth. Unfortunately, you can't explain it that easily to the dog. With adult supervision, they will learn how to play together.

Young children love to tease. Sticking their faces or wiggling their hands or fingers in the dog's face is teasing. To another person it might be just annoying, but it is threatening to a dog. There's another difference: We can make the child stop by an explanation, but the only way a dog can stop it is with a warning growl and then with teeth. Teasing is the major cause of children being bitten by their pets. Treat it seriously.

Older Children

The best age for a child to get a first dog is between the ages of 8 and 12. That's when kids are able to accept some real responsibility for their pet. Even so, take the child's vow of "I will never *ever* forget to feed (brush, walk, etc.) the dog" for what it's worth: a child's good intention at that moment. Most kids today have extra lessons, soccer practice, Little League, ballet, and so forth piled on top of school schedules. There will be many times when Mom will have to come to the dog's rescue. "I walked the dog for you so you can set the table for me" is one way to get around a missed appointment without laying on blame or guilt.

Kids in this age group make excellent obedience trainers because they are into the teaching/learning process themselves and they lack the self-consciousness of adults. Attending a dog show is something the whole family can enjoy, and watching Junior Showmanship may catch the eye of the kids. Older children can begin to get involved in many of the recreational activities that were reviewed in the previous chapter. Some of the agility obstacles, for example, can be set up in the backyard as a family project (with an adult making sure all the equipment is safe and secure for the dog).

Older kids are also beginning to look to the future, and may envision themselves as veterinarians or trainers or show dog handlers or writers of the next Lassie best-seller. Dogs are perfect confidants for these dreams. They won't tell a soul.

Other Pets

Introduce all pets tactfully. In a dog/cat situation, hold the dog, not the cat. Let two dogs meet on neutral turf—a stroll in the park or a walk down the street—with both on loose leads to permit all the normal canine ways of saying hello, including routine sniffing, circling, more sniffing, and so on. Small creatures such as hamsters, chinchillas or mice must be kept safe from their natural predators (dogs and cats).

Festive Family Occasions

Parties are great for people, but not necessarily for
puppies. Until all the guests have arrived, put the dog
in his crate or in a room where he won't be disturbed.
A socialized dog can join the fun later as long as
he's not underfoot, annoying guests or into the hors
d'oeuvres.

There are a few dangers to consider, too. Doors opening and closing can allow a puppy to slip out unnoticed
in the confusion, and you'll be organizing a search
party instead of playing host or hostess. Party food and
buffet service are not for dogs. Let Rufus party in his
crate with a nice big dog biscuit.

At Christmas time, not only are tree decorations dangerous and breakable (and perhaps family heirlooms),
but extreme caution should be taken with the lights,
cords and outlets for the tree lights and any other fes-
tive lighting. Occasionally a dog lifts a leg, ignoring the
fact that the tree is indoors. To avoid this, use a canine
repellent, made for gardens, on the tree. Or keep him
out of the tree room unless supervised. And whatever
you do, *don't* invite trouble by hanging his toys on the
tree!

Car Travel

Before you plan a vacation by car or RV with Rufus, be
sure he enjoys car travel. Nothing spoils a holiday
quicker than a carsick dog! Work within the dog's com-
fort level. Get in the car with the dog in his crate or
attached to a canine car safety belt and just sit there
until he relaxes. That's all. Next time, get in the car,
turn on the engine and go nowhere. Just sit. When that
is okay, turn on the engine and go around the block.
Now you can go for a ride and include a stop where
you get out, leaving the dog for a minute or two.

On a warm day, always park in the shade and leave windows open several inches. And return quickly. It only
takes 10 minutes for a car to become an overheated
steel death trap.

Motel or Pet Motel?

Not all motels or hotels accept pets, but you have a much better choice today than even a few years ago. To find a dog-friendly lodging, look at *On the Road Again With Man's Best Friend*, a series of directories that detail bed and breakfasts, inns, family resorts and other hotels/motels. Some places require a refundable deposit to cover any damage incurred by the dog. More B&Bs accept pets now, but some restrict the size.

If taking Rufus with you is not feasible, check out boarding kennels in your area. Your veterinarian may offer this service, or recommend a kennel or two he or she is familiar with. Go see the facilities for yourself, ask about exercise, diet, housing, and so on. Or, if you'd rather have Rufus stay home, look into bonded petsitters, many of whom will also bring in the mail and water your plants.

chapter 11

Your Dog
and your
Community

by Bardi McLennan

Step outside your home with your dog and you are no longer just family, you are both part of your community. This is when the phrase "responsible pet ownership" takes on serious implications. For starters, it means you pick up after your dog—not just occasionally, but every time your dog eliminates away from home. That means you have joined the Plastic Baggy Brigade! You always have plastic sandwich bags in your pocket and several in the car. It means you teach your kids how to use them, too. If you think this is "yucky," just imagine what the person (a non-doggy person) who inadvertently steps in the mess thinks!

Your responsibility extends to your neighbors: To their ears (no annoying barking); to their property (their garbage, their lawn, their flower beds, their cat—especially their cat); to their kids (on bikes, at play); to their kids' toys and sports equipment.

There are numerous dog-related laws, ranging from simple dog licensing and leash laws to those holding you liable for any physical injury or property damage done by your dog. These laws are in place to protect everyone in the community, including you and your dog. There are town ordinances and state laws which are by no means the same in all towns or all states. Ignorance of the law won't get you off the hook. The time to find out what the laws are where you live is now.

Be sure your dog's license is current. This is not just a good local ordinance, it can make the difference between finding your lost dog or not.

Dressing your dog up makes him appealing to strangers.

Many states now require proof of rabies vaccination and that the dog has been spayed or neutered before issuing a license. At the same time, keep up the dog's annual immunizations.

Never let your dog run loose in the neighborhood. This will not only keep you on the right side of the leash law, it's the outdoor version of the rule about not giving your dog "freedom to get into trouble."

Good Canine Citizen

Sometimes it's hard for a dog's owner to assess whether or not the dog is sufficiently socialized to be accepted by the community at large. Does Rufus or Rufina display good, controlled behavior in public? The AKC's Canine Good Citizen program is available through many dog organizations. If your dog passes the test, the title "CGC" is earned.

The overall purpose is to turn your dog into a good neighbor and to teach you about your responsibility to your community as a dog owner. Here are the ten things your dog must do willingly:

1. Allow a stranger to handle him or her as a groomer or veterinarian would.
2. Accept a stranger stopping to chat with you.
3. Walk nicely on a loose lead.
4. Walk calmly through a crowd.
5. Sit and be petted by a stranger.
6. Sit and down on command.
7. Stay put when you move away.
8. Casually greet another dog.
9. React confidently to distractions.
10. Accept being tied up in a strange place and left alone for a few minutes.

Schools and Dogs

Schools are getting involved with pet ownership on an educational level. It has been proven that children who are kind to animals are humane in their attitude toward other people as adults.

A dog is a child's best friend, and so children are often primary pet owners, if not the primary caregivers. Unfortunately, they are also the ones most often bitten by dogs. This occurs due to a lack of understanding that pets, no matter how sweet, cuddly and loving, are still animals. Schools, along with parents, dog clubs, dog fanciers and the AKC, are working to change all that with video programs for children not only in grade school, but in the nursery school and pre-kindergarten age group. Teaching youngsters how to be responsible dog owners is important community work. When your dog has a CGC, volunteer to take part in an educational classroom event put on by your dog club.

Boy Scout Merit Badge

A Merit Badge for Dog Care can be earned by any Boy
Scout ages 11 to 18. The requirements are not easy, but
amount to a complete course in responsible dog care
and general ownership. Here are just a few of the
things a Scout must do to earn that badge:

Point out ten parts of the dog using the correct
names.

Give a report (signed by parent or guardian) on
your care of the dog (feeding, food used, housing,
exercising, grooming and bathing), plus what has
been done to keep the dog healthy.

Explain the right way to obedience train a dog,
and demonstrate three comments.

Several of the requirements have to do with health
care, including first aid, handling a hurt dog, and
the dangers of home treatment for a serious
ailment.

The final requirement is to know the local laws
and ordinances involving dogs.

There are similar programs for Girl Scouts and 4-H
members.

Local Clubs

Local dog clubs are no longer in existence just to put
on a yearly dog show. Today, they are apt to be the hub
of the community's involvement with pets. Dog clubs
conduct educational forums with big-name speakers,
stage demonstrations of canine talent in a busy mall
and take dogs of various breeds to schools for classroom discussion.

The quickest way to feel accepted as a member in a
club is to volunteer your services! Offer to help with
something—anything—and watch your popularity
(and your interest) grow.

Therapy Dogs

Once your dog has earned that essential CGC and reliably demonstrates a steady, calm temperament, you could look into what therapy dogs are doing in your area.

Therapy dogs go with their owners to visit patients at hospitals or nursing homes, generally remaining on leash but able to coax a pat from a stiffened hand, a smile from a blank face, a few words from sealed lips or a hug from someone in need of love.

Nursing homes cover a wide range of patient care. Some specialize in care of the elderly, some in the treatment of specific illnesses, some in physical therapy. Children's facilities also welcome visits from *Your dog can make a difference in lots of lives.* trained therapy dogs for boosting morale in their pediatric patients. Hospice care for the terminally ill and the at-home care of AIDS patients are other areas where this canine visiting is desperately needed. Therapy dog training comes first.

There is a lot more involved than just taking your nice friendly pooch to someone's bedside. Doing therapy dog work involves your own emotional stability as well as that of your dog. But once you have met all the requirements for this work, making the rounds once a week or once a month with your therapy dog is possibly the most rewarding of all community activities.

Disaster Aid

This community service is definitely not for everyone, partly because it is time-consuming. The initial training is rigorous, and there can be no let-up in the continuing workouts, because members are on call 24 hours a day to go wherever they are needed at a moment's notice. But if you think you would like to be able to assist in a disaster, look into search-and-rescue work. The network of search-and-rescue volunteers is worldwide, and all members of the American Rescue Dog Association (ARDA) who are qualified to do this work are volunteers who train and maintain their own dogs.

Physical Aid

Most people are familiar with Seeing Eye dogs, which serve as blind people's eyes, but not with all the other work that dogs are trained to do to assist the disabled. Dogs are also specially trained to pull wheelchairs, carry school books, pick up dropped objects, open and close doors. Some also are ears for the deaf. All these assistance-trained dogs, by the way, are allowed anywhere "No Pet" signs exist (as are therapy dogs when

properly identified). Getting started in any of this fascinating work requires a background in dog training and canine behavior, but there are also volunteer jobs ranging from answering the phone to cleaning out kennels to providing a foster home for a puppy. You have only to ask.

Making the rounds with your therapy dog can be very rewarding.

part four

Beyond
the
Basics

chapter 12

Recommended Reading

Books

GENERAL

American Kennel Club (AKC). *American Kennel Club Dog Care and Training.* New York: Howell Book House, 1991.

————. *The Complete Dog Book,* 19th Edition Revised. New York: Howell Book House, 1998.

Bamberger, Michelle, DVM. *Help! The Quick Guide to First Aid for Your Dog.* New York: Howell Book House, 1995.

Carlson, Liisa, DVM, and James Giffin, MD. *Dog Owners Home Veterinary Handbook,* 3rd Edition. New York: Howell Book House, 1999.

DeBitetto, James, DVM, and Sarah Hodgson. *You & Your Puppy.* New York: Howell Book House, 2000.

Rogers Clark, Anne, and Andrew H. Brace. *The International Encyclopedia of Dogs.* New York: Howell Book House, 1995.

Vella, Bob, and Ken Leebow. *300 Incredible Things for Pet Lovers on the Internet.* Marietta, Georgia: 300 Incredible.com, 2000.

Volhard, Wendy, and Kerry Brown, DVM. *Holistic Guide for a Healthy Dog.* New York: Howell Book House, 2000.

ABOUT DOG SHOWS

Alston, George. *The Winning Edge.* New York: Howell Book House, 1992.

Hall, Lynn. *Dog Showing for Beginners.* New York: Howell Book House, 1994.

About Training

Arden, Andrea. *Dog-Friendly Dog Training*. New York: Howell Book House, 1999.

Benjamin, Carol Lea. *Dog Training for Kids*. New York: Howell Book House, 1988.

———. *Dog Training in 10 Minutes*. New York: Howell Book House, 1997.

Burch, Mary, PhD, and Jon Bailey. *How Dogs Learn*. New York: Howell Book House, 1999.

Dunbar, Ian, PhD, MRCVS. *Dog Behavior: An Owner's Guide to a Happy Healthy Pet*. New York: Howell Book House, 1996.

———. *How to Teach a New Dog Old Tricks*. James & Kenneth Publishers, 1998. Order from the publisher at 2140 Shattuck Ave. #2406, Berkeley, CA 94704. (510) 658-8588.

Evans, Job Michael. *People, Pooches and Problems*. New York: Howell Book House, 2001.

Hodgson, Sarah. *Dogperfect: The User Friendly Guide to a Well Behaved Dog*. New York: Howell Book House, 1995.

New Skete Monks. *How to Be Your Dog's Best Friend*. Boston: Little Brown & Company, 1978.

Pryor, Karen. *Don't Shoot the Dog! The New Art of Teaching and Training*, Revised Edition. New York: Bantam Doubleday Dell, 1999.

Rutherford, Clarice, and David H. Neil, MRCVS. *How to Raise a Puppy You Can Live With*. Loveland, Colorado: Alpine Publications, 1982.

Volhard, Jack, and Melissa Bartlett. *What All Good Dogs Should Know: The Sensible Way to Train*. New York: Howell Book House, 1991.

About Breeding

Finder Harris, Beth J. *Breeding a Litter: The Complete Book of Prenatal and Postnatal Care*. New York: Howell Book House, 1993.

Holst, Phyllis. *Canine Reproduction: The Breeder's Guide*. Loveland, Colorado: Alpine Publications, 1999.

Walkowicz, Chris, and Bonnie Wilcox, DVM. *Successful Dog Breeding: The Complete Handbook of Canine Midwifery*. New York: Howell Book House, 1994.

American Rescue Dog Association. *Search and Rescue Dogs.* New York: Howell Book House, 1991.

Barwig, Susan, and Stewart Hilliard. *Schutzhund.* New York: Howell Book House, 1991.

Burch, Mary. *Volunteering with Your Pet.* New York: Howell Book House, 1996.

O'Neil, Jacqueline F. *All About Agility.* New York: Howell Book House, 1999.

Vollhard, Jack and Wendy. *The Canine Good Citizen.* New York: Howell Book House, 1994.

Magazines

The AKC GAZETTE, The Official Journal for the Sport of Purebred Dogs
American Kennel Club
260 Madison Avenue
New York, NY 10016
(212) 696-8200
www.akc.org

The Bark
2810 8th Street
Berkeley, CA 94710
(510) 704-0827
www.thebark.com

Dog Fancy
Fancy Publications
3 Burroughs
Irvine, CA 92718
(949) 855-8822
www.animalnetwork.com

Dog & Kennel
Pet Publishing, Inc.
7-L Dundas Circle
Greensboro, NC 27407
(336) 292-4047
www.dogandkennel.com

Dog Watch Newsletter
P.O. Box 420235
Palm Coast, FL 32142-0235
(800) 829-5574
www.vet.cornell.edu/publicresources/dog

Dog World
Primedia
500 North Dearborn, Suite 1100
Chicago, IL 60610
(877) 224-7711
www.dogworldmag.com

Videos

"SIRIUS Puppy Training," by Ian Dunbar, PhD, MRCVS. James & Kenneth Publishers, 2140 Shattuck Ave. #2406, Berkeley, CA 94704. Order from the publisher.

"Training the Companion Dog," from Dr. Dunbar's British TV Series, James & Kenneth Publishers. (See address above.)

The American Kennel Club produces videos on every breed of dog, as well as on hunting tests, field trials and other areas of interest to purebred dog owners. For more information, write to AKC/Video Fulfillment, 5580 Centerview Dr., Suite 200, Raleigh, NC 27606. The AKC can be reached at (919) 233-9767, or visit its Web site at www.akc.org.

chapter 13

Resources

Breed Clubs and Registries

Registry organizations register purebred dogs. The American Kennel Club is the oldest and largest in the United States, and currently recognizes over 130 breeds. The United Kennel Club registers some breeds the AKC doesn't (including the American Pit Bull Terrier and the Miniature Fox Terrier), as well as many of the same breeds. The other clubs included here are for your reference; the AKC can provide you with a list of foreign registries.

Every breed recognized by the American Kennel Club has a national (parent) club. National clubs are a great source of information on your breed. You can get the name of the secretary of the club by contacting:

American Kennel Club (AKC)
260 Madison Avenue, 4th Floor
New York, NY 10016
(212) 696-8200
www.akc.org

For breeder referrals, call the customer service department in North Carolina at (919) 233-9767, or visit their Web site.

United Kennel Club (UKC)
100 East Kilgore Road
Portage, MI 49002-5584
(616) 343-9020
www.ukcdogs.com

American Rare Breed Association (ARBA)
9921 Frank Tippet Road
Cheltenham, MD 20612
(301) 868-5718
www.arba.org

155

Canadian Kennel Club (CKC)
89 Skyway Avenue
Etobicoke, Ontario
Canada M9W 6R4
(800) 250-8040
(416) 675-5511
information@ckc.ca

Health Registries

CERF
Department of Veterinary Clinical Science
School of Veterinary Medicine
Purdue University
West Lafayette, IN 47907
(765) 494-8179
yshen@vet.purdue.edu

Orthopedic Foundation for Animals (OFA)
2300 East Nifong Boulevard
Columbia, MO 65201-3856
(573) 442-0418
ofa@ofa.org
(Hip registry)

Activity Clubs

Write to the following organizations for information on the
activities they sponsor.

American Kennel Club (AKC)
260 Madison Avenue, 4th Floor
New York, NY 10016
(212) 696-8200
www.akc.org
(Conformation Shows, Obedience Trials, Field Trials and
Hunting Tests, Agility, Canine Good Citizen, Lure Coursing,
Herding, Tracking, Earthdog Tests, Coonhunting)

United Kennel Club (UKC)
100 East Kilgore Road
Portage, MI 49002-5584
(616) 343-9020
www.ukcdogs.com
(Conformation Shows, Obedience Trials, Agility, Hunting
for Various Breeds, Terrier Trials and more)

North American Flyball Association
1400 West Devon Avenue, #152
Chicago, IL 60660
www.flyball.org

Trainers

Association of Pet Dog Trainers
66 Morris Avenue, Suite 2A
Springfield, NJ 07081
(800) PET-DOGS
www.apdp.com

National Association of Dog Obedience Instructors
2286 East Steel Road
St. Johns, MI 48879
www.nadoi.org

Dog Friendly Web Sites

The following Web sites offer a variety of experiences for the dog-loving Internet surfer. Some sites present specific breed information, while others provide quizzes and question-naires to help you decide which dog breed is the best one for you and your family. You can view photographs, research breeders and rescue organizations in your area, find out the best ways to exercise or travel with your pet or just discover more about *canis familiaris*. Enjoy!

Dog Breed Information Center
www.dogbreedinfo.com
This is a well-designed site with cute doggie graphics and easy-to-use links. Log on to donate toys to rescue organiza-tions, post messages for like-minded dog folk, take question-naires to discover which dog breed is best suited to your family and your home, view a plethora of canine photographs or discover the answers to frequently asked dog-care and -training questions.

Choosing the Perfect Dog
www.choosingtheperfectdog.net
Another good, all-purpose site for dog owners or dog-owner wannabes. Information is presented in a very organized man-ner, with helpful sidebars and links. Practical answers are given to questions such as "How do I match a dog to my lifestyle?" Or "How much time/money/stuff do I need to provide for a dog?" The site prompts visitors to think carefully about getting a dog, and to responsibly research dog breeds so that everyone involved lives happily ever after.

Good News for Pets
www.goodnewsforpets.com
This weekly digest provides interesting tidbits on all things canine related. It profiles people who are active in the dog community, provides nutrition facts, addresses legal issues

and focuses attention on how dogs are portrayed in books and on film. Visit every Monday for the "Pet Question of the Week."

Dog Advisors
www.dogadvisors.com

This is a fun site where the fancier can delve a little deeper and learn a little more about his or her favorite dog breeds. Different breeds are highlighted at various times, as are specific breeders.

United States Dog Agility Association, Inc. (USDAA)
www.usdaa.com

This USDAA is an international site that gives visitors the opportunity to find out the latest news in the world of agility training. It provides an events calendar, records titles and tournaments, defines performance standards and lists affiliated groups. "Front Page News" is updated on a weekly basis.

Canine Freestyle Federation, Inc.
www.canine-freestyle.org

Welcome to the world of Canine Freestyle—or doggie dancing, if you will. Canine freestyle is performed by dog and trainer in a ring, and all moves are choreographed to music. To learn more, visit this well-designed, comprehensive Web site. The CFF also maintains records of freestyle events and publishes a newsletter.

Pets Welcome
www.petswelcome.com

If you plan on travelling with your pet, a visit to this site is a must. The listings page offers information on over 25,000 hotels, bed & breakfasts, ski resorts, campgrounds and pet-friendly beaches. Plenty of advice and knowledge are provided for those who can't imagine leaving their pet at home.

Vet Info.com
www.vetinfo.com

If your dog is suffering from a particular ailment, you can find out more about it by visiting vetinfo.com. The format of this site is easy to use, with each disease listed in alphabetical order. To delve even deeper into your pet's health, you might subscribe to *Vetinfo Digest* for its "Ask Dr. Mike" Segment.